WINE ENTHUSIAST
M A G A Z I N E

POCKET GUIDE TO

WINE

www.winemag.com

RUNNING PRESS
PHILADELPHIA · LONDON

9   8   7   6   5   4   3   2
Digit on the right indicates the number of this printing

Library of Congress Control Number: 2006900799
ISBN-13: 978-0-7624-2751-2
ISBN-10: 0-7624-2751-5

Cover design by Bill Jones
Interior design by Rosemary Tottoroto
Edited by Diana C. von Glahn
Photo research by Susan Oyama
Typography: Adobe Garamond and Bureau Grotesque

This book may be ordered by mail from the publisher.
Please include $2.50 for postage and handling.
But try your bookstore first!

Running Press Book Publishers
2300 Chestnut Street
Philadelphia, Pennsylvania 19103-4371
Visit us on the web!
www.runningpress.com
www.runningpresscooks.com
www.winemag.com

Preface

AT *Wine Enthusiast Magazine*, WE'RE ALL ABOUT the enjoyment of wine. And to us, enjoyment is a two-pronged process: Part one is the "relax, drink what you like, don't worry about what anyone thinks" portion of the program; part two is the "experiment, try something new" portion, because wine lends itself to that approach. There are so many grape varieties, blends, countries (with  their varied climates and soils), and producers that it is a world you can spend a lifetime exploring.

This is a great guide to that lifelong activity. If you're intimidated by wine—buying it at retail, ordering it at a restaurant—inside this book you'll find all the information you need to be comfortable with the subject. Profiles of wine regions and grape varieties, tips on tasting and storing, a glossary of terms—we fit so much solid information in this pocket-size book, I'm sure you're feeling less intimidated already! And if you're comfortable enough with your wine knowledge to realize you don't know it all, you may find some interesting reading here.

No matter what your level of wine familiarity, we encourage you to visit www.winemag.com for our easy-to-use wine database. Updated regularly, the database is an indispensable guide to the world's wines—you'll have a description, price, and our panelists' score of thousands of wines at the click of a key.

Welcome to the world of wine. Once you start enjoying wine with some thought given to what has gone into that glass, you will be a lifelong enthusiast.

Cheers,

Adam Strum
Publisher and Editor-in-Chief
Wine Enthusiast Magazine

Contents

CHAPTER ONE

The ABC's of Tasting

LEARNING TO TASTE WINE IS NO DIFFERENT than learning to appreciate music or art—the pleasure you receive is proportionate to the effort you make. The more you fine-tune your sensory abilities, the better you are able to understand and enjoy the nuances and details that great wines express. The time and effort invested in palate training is very rewarding. It's also a whole lot of fun!

Many people feel a bit clueless when it comes to wine. It's a vast and complicated subject, and much of its pleasure comes from identifying the various scents and flavors that combine to create each wine's unique personality. But how much attention do we pay to developing our senses of smell and taste?

The ability to sniff out and untangle the subtle threads that weave into complex wine aromas is essential for tasting. Try holding your nose while you swallow a mouthful of wine; you will find that most of the flavor is muted. Your nose is the key to your palate. Once you learn how to give wine a good sniff, you'll begin to develop the ability to isolate flavors—to notice the way they unfold and interact—and (to some degree) to assign language to describe them.

This is exactly what wine professionals—those who make, sell, buy, and write about wine—are able to do. For any wine enthusiast, it is the pay-off for all the effort.

This little book is designed to get you started and give you some guidelines for your ongoing exploration of wine. We have tried to keep it simple, logical, and smart. It's a map to discover your own palate. There is no right or wrong way to learn to taste, but some "rules" do apply.

First and foremost, you need to be methodical and focused. Find a consistent approach that you can follow regularly. Not every single glass or bottle of wine must be analyzed in this way, of course. But if you really want to learn about wine, a certain amount of dedicated, ongoing effort is required. Make a habit of taking just a minute, whenever you have a glass of wine in your hand, to stop all conversation and shut out all distraction and focus your attention on the appearance, the scents, the flavors and the finish of the wine.

You can run through this mental checklist in a

minute or less, and it will quickly help you to plot out the compass points of your palate. Of course, sipping a chilled Rosé from a paper cup at a garden party does not require the same effort as diving into a well-aged Bordeaux served from a Riedel Sommelier series glass. But those are the extreme ends of the spectrum. Just about everything you are likely to encounter falls somewhere in between.

You have probably heard many times, from both friends and experts, that any wine you like is a good wine. This is true if your goal is simply to enjoy wine. Then, you don't have to do more than take a sip, give it a swallow, and let your inner geek say "yes" or "no." End of job.

But quickly passing judgment is not the same as truly under-standing and evaluating wine. Learning to taste properly means that you can identify the main flavor and scent components in every wine you try. It means that you know the basic characteristics for all of the most important varietal grapes, and beyond that, for the blended wines from the world's best wine-producing regions. And you can also quickly point out specific flaws in bad wines.

Rest assured, there are some truly bad wines out there, and not all of them are inexpensive. Some flaws are the result of bad winemaking; others are caused by bad corks or poor storage. If you are ordering a nice bottle of wine in a restaurant, you want to be certain that the wine you receive tastes the way it was intended to taste. Not every server in every restaurant can be relied upon to notice and replace a wine that is corked, for example. You are ultimately the one who will be asked to approve the bottle. Being able to sniff out common faults such as trichloroanisole (TCA) (see Glossary) will certainly make it easier to send a wine back.

Setting the Scene

So, how do you evaluate a glass of wine?

First, make note of any circumstances surrounding your wine tasting that may affect your impressions. A noisy or crowded room makes concentration difficult. Cooking smells, perfumes, even pets can destroy your ability to get a clear sense of a wine's aromas. A glass that is too small, the wrong shape, or smells of detergent or dust can also affect the wine's flavor.

The temperature of the wine will also have an impact on your impressions. So will the age of the wine, and any residual flavors from whatever else you have been eating or drinking. As much as possible, neutralize the tasting conditions, so the wine has a fair chance to stand on its own.

Even at a crowded wine tasting it is usually possible to find a quiet corner and contemplate the contents of your glass undisturbed. If a wine is served too cold, warm it by cupping the bowl of the glass with your hands. If a glass seems musty, give it a quick rinse with wine, not water, swirling it around to cover all the sides of the bowl. This is called conditioning the glass. Finally, if there are strong aromas nearby—especially perfume—walk as far away from them as you can and try to find some neutral air.

Evaluating by Sight

Once your tasting conditions are as close to neutral as possible, quickly examine the wine. The glass should be about one-third full. First, look straight down into the glass, then hold the glass up to the light, and finally, give it a tilt, so the wine rolls toward the edges of the glass. This will allow you to see the wine's complete color range, not just the dark center.

Looking down, you get a sense of the depth of color, which gives a clue to the density and saturation of the wine. You will also learn to identify certain varietal grapes by color and scent. If you're tasting a red wine, a deeply-saturated, purple-black color might well be Syrah or Zinfandel, while a lighter, pale brick shade would suggest Pinot Noir or Sangiovese.

Viewing the wine through the side of the glass held in front of a light shows you how clear it is. A murky wine might have chemical or fermentation problems. On the other hand, it might just be a wine that was unfiltered or has developed some sediment and got shaken up while being poured. A wine that looks clear and brilliant, and shows some sparkle, is always a good sign.

Tilting the glass so the wine thins out toward the rim will provide clues to the wine's age and weight. If the color looks pale and watery near its edge, it suggests a thin, possibly insipid wine. If the color looks tawny or brown (for a white wine) or orange or rusty brick (for a red wine) it is either an older wine or a wine that has been oxidized and may be past its prime.

Finally, give the glass a good swirl. You can swirl it most easily by keeping it firmly on a flat surface; open air "freestyle" swirling is not recommended for beginners! Notice if the wine forms "legs" or "tears" that run down the sides of the glass. Wines that have good legs are wines with higher alcohol and glycerin content, which generally indicates that they are bigger, riper, more mouth-filling and dense than those that do not.

Evaluating by Sniff

Now you're ready to take a good sniff of the wine. Don't bury your nose inside it. You want to hover over the top like a helicopter pilot surveying rush-hour traffic. Take a series of quick, short sniffs; then step away and let the information filter through to your brain.

There are many guidelines to help you train your nose to identify key wine fragrances, both good and bad. There are potentially thousands of aroma components in a glass of good wine, so forget about finding them all. Naming all the fruits and flowers and herbs and other scents you can trowel out of the glass can be a fun game, but it is not essential to enjoying and evaluating a wine.

First, look for off-aromas that indicate a wine is spoiled. A wine that is corked (*see* Glossary) will smell like a musty old attic or mushrooms and taste like a wet newspaper. This is a terminal, unfixable flaw. A wine that has been bottled with a strong dose of SO_2 will smell like burnt matches; this will blow off if you give it a bit of vigorous swirling. A smell of vinegar indicates VA (volatile acidity) (*see* Glossary); a nail-polish smell is ethyl acetate. Different people have different tolerances for both the burnt-matches and vinegar aromas, and in small doses these aromas can actually contribute to a wine's complexity. But they should never dominate. The same can be said of *brettanomyces*, an undesirable yeast that reeks of sweaty saddles. A little bit of "brett" gives red wines an earthy, leathery component; too much obliterates all the flavors of fruit. Identifying these common flaws is at least as important as reciting the names of all the fruits and flowers. And it will also help you to understand your own palate sensitivities and blind spots.

If there are no obvious off-aromas, look for fruit aromas. Wine is made from grapes, so it should smell like fresh fruit, unless it is very old, very sweet, or very cold. You can learn to look for specific fruits for specific grapes, and many grapes will show a spectrum of possible fruit scents that help you to identify the growing conditions—cool climate, moderate or very warm—of the vineyard. (*See* Chapter Four for more details.)

Next, look for other plant aromas: flowers, leaves, herbs, spices, stems, and vegetables. Floral aromas are particularly common in cool-climate white wines such as Riesling and Gewürztraminer, and some Rhône varietals such as Viognier. Some other grapes can be expected to carry herbal or grassy scents. Sauvignon Blanc is often strongly grassy, while Cabernet Sauvignon can be scented with herbs and hints of vegetation. Rhône reds often show delightful scents of Provençal herbs. Most people prefer that any herbal aromas be delicate. The best wine aromas are complex but balanced, specific but harmonious.

Another group of common wine aromas might be characterized as "earthy." Scents of mushroom, damp earth, leather, and rock occur in many red wines. A little mushroomy smell can add nuance; it can also suggest a possible grape or place of origin for the wine if you are tasting the wine blind. Too much mushroom may mean that the grapes failed to ripen sufficiently, or were from an inferior clone. The scent of horse or tack-room leather can be an accent, but too much can indicate brettanomyces. Scents of earth, mineral, and rock sometimes occur in the very finest white and red wines; these can be indications of *terroir*—the particular conditions of the vineyard that are expressed as specific scents and flavors in the finished wine.

If you smell toast, smoke, vanilla, chocolate, espresso, roasted nuts, or even caramel in a wine, you are most likely picking up scents from aging in new oak barrels. Depending upon a multitude of factors, including the type of oak, the way the barrels were made, the age of the barrels, the level of char, and the way the winemaker has mixed and matched them, barrels can impart a vast array of scents and flavors to finished wines. Think of the barrels as a winemaker's color palette, to be used the way a painter uses tubes of paint.

Finally, there are smells that relate to the way a wine was made and its age. Young white wines and young sparkling wines, for example, may have a scent very reminiscent of beer; this is from the yeast. Some dessert wines smell strongly of honey; this is evidence of *botrytis cinerea*

(*see* Glossary), often called *noble rot*, and is typical of the very greatest Sauternes. Chardonnays that smell of buttered popcorn or caramel have likely been put through a secondary, malolactic fermentation, which converts malic to lactic acids, softening the wines and opening up the aromas.

Older wines evolve more complex, less fruity aromas. A fully mature wine can offer an explosion of highly nuanced scents, beautifully co-mingled and virtually impossible to name. It's pure pleasure; no need to put words to it.

Nonetheless, the effort to put words to wine aromas helps you focus on, understand, and retain your impressions of different wines. You want to build a memory bank of wine smells and their meanings. That is where the language of wine can add value to a wine-tasting event. Learning to talk the talk, if not carried to extremes, helps to dispel some wine myths, such as the confusion surrounding descriptions on wine labels. So while a Gewürztraminer may taste of grapefruit and a Zinfandel of raspberries, you know that these are simply descriptive terms.

Evaluating by Taste

Finally, it's time to taste! Take a sip—not a large swallow—of wine into your mouth and suck on it as if pulling it through a straw. Ignore the stares of those around you; sucking in air aerates the wine and circulates it throughout your mouth. You want the wine to hit as many of your taste receptors as possible, so you can truly enjoy the wine's complexities.

Again, you'll encounter a wide range of fruit, flower, herb, mineral, barrel, and other flavors, and if you've done your sniffing homework, most will follow right along where the aromas left off. Aside from simply identifying flavors,

you are also using your taste buds to determine if the wine is balanced, harmonious, complex, evolved, and complete.

A balanced wine should have its basic flavor components in good proportion. Our taste buds detect sweet, sour, salty, and bitter. Sweet (residual sugar) and sour (acidity) are obviously important components of wine. Saltiness is rarely encountered, and bitterness should be more a feeling of astringency (from tannins) than actual bitter flavors. Most dry wines will display a mix of flavors derived from the aromas, along with the tastes of the acids, tannins, and alcohol, which cannot generally be detected simply by smell. There is no single formula for all wines, but there should always be balance between the flavors. If a wine is too sour, too sugary, too astringent, too hot (alcoholic), too bitter, or too flabby (lack of acid) then it is not a well-balanced wine. If it is young, is not likely to age well; if it is old, it may be falling apart or perhaps completely gone.

A harmonious wine has all of its flavors seamlessly integrated. It's quite possible, especially in young wines, for all the components to be present in the wine in good proportion, but they stick out. The individual components can be identified easily, but you can feel all the edges; they have not blended together. It's a sign of very good winemaking when a young wine has already come together and presents its flavors harmoniously.

Complexity can mean many things. Your ability to detect and appreciate complexity in wine will become a good gauge of your overall progress. The simplest flavors to recognize—very ripe, jammy fruit and strong vanilla flavors from various oak treatments—are reminiscent of soft drinks. It is perfectly natural for new wine drinkers to relate to them first, because they are familiar and likeable. Some extremely successful wine brands have been formulated to offer these flavors in abundance. But they do not offer complexity.

Complex wines seem to dance in your mouth. They change, even as you are tasting them. They are like good paintings; the more you look at them the more there is to see. In older wines, these complexities sometimes evolve to the realm of the sublime. The length of a wine, whether old or young, is one good indication of complexity—simply note how long the flavors linger after you swallow. You might even try looking at your watch if you have a particularly interesting wine in your glass. Most beginning wine drinkers move on too quickly to the next sip when a really good wine is in the glass. Hold on! Let the wine finish its dance before you change partners.

A complete wine is balanced, harmonious, complex, and evolved, with a lingering, satisfying finish. Such wines deserve extra attention, because they have more to offer, in terms of both pleasure and training, than any others you will taste.

Setting up Tastings

You will learn most quickly and effectively when you taste a group of wines—at least six, no more than twelve—arranged by similarity. Taste wines that have some things in common—the same grape and region, for example—but are made by different winemakers.

Whenever possible, taste with someone who knows more about wine than you do. Don't let that person dictate your tastes, but let them guide you and point out things that you might otherwise miss. Many wine shops offer free or inexpensive tastings, and their owners are usually good wine guides.

A good way to begin your research into wine is by learning to identify varietal character (*see* Glossary). There are roughly a dozen truly important white wine grapes, and an equal number of must-know red wine grapes. Pick one that you already know you like, such as Chardonnay or Merlot, and focus your tastings on examples of that grape from all over the world. This will help you to find the specific scents and flavors that are the varietal characteristics of that grape, wherever it is grown. Work grape by grape, or region by region, to assemble your "library" of palate impressions and preferences.

CHAPTER TWO

Getting the Most from Wine

HERE'S A SIMPLE EXPERIMENT YOU CAN TRY at home and amaze your friends. Select a favorite bottle of white wine and another of red. Set out three or four different glasses for each person. For example, you might use a big, bowl-shaped wine glass, a small, thick-rimmed glass, a simple tumbler, and anything else that you have in your cupboard. Then have everyone take a small taste of each wine from each glass.

Believe it or not, even a modestly decent wine will taste different in every glass! Some glasses will mute the flavor, some will emphasize odd scents, some will have no scents at all. If you are fortunate, one glass will present the wine perfectly, and everyone will agree that this is how the wine is supposed to taste. This is a wine fact that almost defies belief—until you try it for yourself.

When you pour a great wine into a not-so-great glass, it turns into a very ordinary wine. This happens quite frequently in restaurants, but you may also encounter bad stemware at wineries, at public tastings, and at dinner parties. Out comes a terrific bottle of wine, and it's served in a glass that is too small, too thick, colored blue or green, stained or smelling of detergent. Under these bad conditions, you won't be able to discern the true flavor offered by the wine.

Insisting on a good glass is not snobbery; it's common sense. If you want to get all the flavor out of every wine you pour, whether it cost you ten dollars or one hundred dollars, you owe it to yourself to invest in good stemware. It does not have to be terribly expensive to be good.

There are now specific glasses made for every major varietal and region in the world, and they do work. But don't panic. It's not necessary to stock up on them all. You'll do just fine with a few well-chosen glasses matched to your own wine buying, drinking, and entertaining habits.

What you need will depend upon the type of entertaining you do and the quality of the wines you serve. For a picnic or deck party, at which you will be pouring simple wines from current vintages, a couple dozen clear glass tumblers may suffice. For better wines and more formal tastings or intimate dinner gatherings, you'll want a selection of stemware that allows each guest a flute-

shaped glass for sparkling wines, a tapered, ten- to twelve-ounce glass for white wines, and a larger, rounder glass for red wines.

Avoid colored glass, even if just the stem is tinted. You want to be able to see the wine's own color. If you use a dishwasher, run the glasses through using hot water only; don't use detergent. Toss out those tiny, thick-lipped glasses with the rolled rims; use tumblers instead. Remember, size matters. Your glass should be large enough to hold three or four ounces of wine without being more than one third full. You need the air space to properly display the wine's aroma. Remember, aroma = flavor!

The right glassware is the single most important aspect to setting yourself up for a good tasting experience. Close behind is serving your wines at the right temperature. Whether white or red, wines that are too cold will lose all aromas and much flavor. Wines that are too warm may lose their crispness and turn flabby and volatile; heat also intensifies the impression of alcohol. Sparkling wines and sweet dessert wines are served at cooler temperatures, to be sure. But they, too, can be over-chilled, causing their aromas to be muted and their flavors to be less detailed.

Over the course of a tasting, wines will slowly warm up, so it is not a bad idea to start them out on the cool side. For dry white wines, rosés, or very light reds, such as Beaujolais, this means around forty-five degrees—about twenty minutes in the fridge will be just about right. For red wines, just a bit above cellar temperature, roughly fifty-eight to sixty degrees Fahrenheit, is the best starting point. Sparkling wines and sweet dessert wines can be chilled in the fridge for an hour or more before being served.

It's not a good idea to put your whites or reds in an ice bucket unless they are way too warm and you need to chill them quickly. Wine responds best to gentle treatment. Whenever possible, try to plan ahead, allowing sufficient time to bring the wine to its proper serving temperature gradually. A regulated wine cellar, or better yet, a wine cooler with variable temperature controls, will do the job well. You will be rewarded with appealing scents and flavors from the moment the cork is pulled until the last glass is drained.

CHAPTER THREE

Wine-Buying Strategies

Smart Wine Buying Takes Planning

In America, most wine is consumed the night it is bought. Whether it is a bottle of Opus One for a dinner party or a box of White Zin to improve Tuesday-night leftovers, it's often opened immediately with little thought.

Unfortunately, buying wine that way sacrifices a great deal of the pleasure of wine, and rarely provides the best deal. Pretentious though it may seem, it's worthwhile to develop a strategy for acquiring wine. It's both fun and rewarding.

There are a number of reasons for planning your purchases, but they almost all lead to having a supply on hand, ideally in a wine cellar or refrigerated storage cabinet. The most obvious advantage is that some wines improve with age, and even if you can  afford to buy properly aged vintages, they may be very difficult to find. Buying young saves money, but also means that you'll be able to enjoy the wine when it's at its peak.

Of course, most wine doesn't improve with age, but if you're reading this, you most likely appreciate the wine that does. Most better reds certainly improve for a few years, and though many of today's wines are made to reach their peaks within a decade, most are released when they're only two or three years old. Hold them for even three or four years and they will improve tremendously. But if you buy wines at that peak stage, you will have to pay a premium.

Serious collectors, of course, often see wine as an investment that can be sold at an appreciated value in the future. Others see the real value in having far better wines to drink themselves.

Of course, some wines just keep on improving for decades: top Bordeaux, Burgundies, Napa Cabs, Barolos, and many Spanish wines fall in this category. It's not wise to drink them when they're only a few years old; if you do, they probably won't be much better than ordinary wines. Some people even develop a taste for old wines that many would consider past their prime, while others enjoy learning what happens to wines as they age.

You can obviously save a great deal when you cellar wines yourself, but even cursory planning can also save a lot of money. Buying wine on sale can be very rewarding. Almost every retailer offers at least ten percent off for full cases, sometimes mixed cases, and that's like getting more than a bottle free with each case.

Some wines are even sold as futures. This primarily applies to top labels, but even some relatively modest wineries sell wine this way if it's in short supply. For example, after disastrous fires and earthquakes in wine warehouses, some producers in California offered attractive futures for their wines to maintain cash flow.

When all is said and done, however, perhaps the best reason for planning ahead is to have the right wine on hand when you want it. It's awful nice to be able to go into your cellar and grab a perfectly aged bottle that's the perfect match for dinner, or to take a special treat to a celebration without a trip to the wine store. In many areas, finding a special bottle could require ordering ahead, or a long drive to a state-controlled liquor store that is open during limited hours.

The only downside to having good wines on hand is a mixed one: You're more likely to enjoy it!

What Do You Like?

Of course, it doesn't make much sense to have a cellar full of wine you don't like. Wine-buying guides provide good reference points for wines you've never tasted, but you'll probably want to. Buy only one bottle of a wine you haven't tasted, instead of many, even if the producer has a good reputation or a well-known reviewer has awarded it a high score. Reputation and wine scores should be starting points, since people's tastes differ widely. Fortunately, there are a lot of ways to help guide your purchases.

One way to improve your odds is to learn which reviewers have tastes that mirror yours. For example, if you love massive Cabernets, which are extremely full-bodied and high in alcohol, find which critics rave over them. Also learn which reviewers prefer more restrained wines that might be more suitable for enjoying with food.

All that said, the best way to learn what you like is by tasting wine. Take wine-tasting classes at wine stores or

local colleges and adult schools. Attend wine events where you can taste a wide variety of wines. Try wines by the glass when available at restaurants and bars. Wine clubs and tasting parties with friends can be both great fun and very informative. Take recommendations from friends, but be sure to consider whether their tastes are similar to yours. Whatever you do, pay attention and take notes. And don't forget to spit (at a tasting, not at a restaurant!) otherwise, all the wine will taste great!

You'll almost always find some surprises, particularly with some inexpensive wines. Most important, accept your own tastes. Drinking wine isn't about forcing yourself to learn to like wines that don't suit you. Remember, above all of the terminology and technicality, the most important thing about wine should be the ability to get the most out of every glass, so you actually enjoy what you're drinking. Drink—and buy—what you like and don't apologize or try to impress others.

Making the Purchase

Once you've decided what wine you like, buy more of it. Although wine choices were once very limited, and still are in some states, in most areas, choices have multiplied, and expand daily as restrictive laws fall to lawsuits or change to reflect today's attitudes and to increase tax revenues.

The old-time wine store—and its modern counterpart—remains one of the best places to buy wines. Clerks in these stores tend to be knowledgeable about wine, and if you become a regular, they can learn more about your

tastes and steer you toward wines you'll likely enjoy. Many shops now offer classes, wine tastings, and other events, and some will even order special wines or ship and deliver them to your home.

In many states, you can buy wine in supermarkets, giant discounters, club stores, discount wine and liquor outlets, and even convenience stores. And they're not just selling basic wine, either. Costco has emerged as one of the nation's largest retailers of fine wines including some that cost hundreds of dollars a bottle.

With barriers to interstate shipping of wine falling, direct purchases from wineries are making more and more sense. While it hardly pays to buy widely distributed wines direct from the wineries and pay shipping when you can buy the same wine at a neighborhood store, often for less, the only place to get some wines is from the winery. This includes special bottles from big producers, including limited production bottlings and library wines (*see* Glossary).

For these wines, the most fun of all is to visit the winery, where you can taste before buying. As wineries spring up all over the country, that may not require a trip to Napa Valley. Many wineries also sell directly over the Internet, by brochure or mail, or by phone, and many independent firms sell wines from many producers as well.

If you're especially fond of certain wineries' wines, it can be fun to sign up for their wine clubs. They typically send a few bottles to members a few times a year, generally at a discount, often including wines not available except to club members or at the winery. Most wine clubs have special events, too, often at the wineries but some in other locations.

Whatever you do, don't forget the wine once it's in your cellar. While some wines improve with age, most don't.

CHAPTER FOUR

Varietal Characteristics

THROUGHOUT EUROPE, WINES ARE CLASSIFIED by vineyard, village, and/or region where they are made. This appellation system is based on precisely defined wine regions, some as small as a single vineyard. As a result, European wine labels feature place names that are closely identified with the grape variety used to make the wine.

Outside Europe, grape (varietal) names have become the primary method of labeling wines. The introduction of varietal wines in California in the decades following Prohibition was a great leap forward, providing consumers with specific information about the grape or grapes in each bottle of wine. A California "Hearty Burgundy" can be made from anything, including Concord grapes, but a wine labeled "Pinot Noir" or "Chardonnay" must be made up of at least seventy-five percent of the named grape. The rest of the blend can be anything the winemaker chooses.

Today, California-style varietal labeling has become so popular that many European wines are using it as well. Most of the every day wines on retail shelves are varietal wines. So it is helpful to learn to identify the generally accepted baseline flavors and aromas of each of the principal grapes. When you read that a wine is "varietally true," it means that it shows the scents and flavors associated with the named grape.

Of course, the same grape grown in different places will reveal different sides of its personality, and winemakers may enhance the natural grape flavors with special yeasts and by storing the wine in barrels. But each of the world's major, important grapes has its own distinctive varietal characteristics. Here are the ones you should know.

White Wine Grapes
CHARDONNAY
Flavors: Green apple, citrus, pineapple, papaya
Versatile and popular, Chardonnay grows all over the world. It reaches its mineral-laced pinnacle in Burgundy, ripens to tropical richness in California and Australia, and takes very well to new oak. It picks up buttery aromas from malolactic fermentation (*see* Glossary) and toasty or vanilla scents from aging in new barrels. By itself, young

Chardonnay is most likely to recall fresh green apples in both smell and flavor. Depending upon the winemaker, it can be made to be crisp and stony, buttery and toasty, or brilliantly fresh with green apple and citrus flavors.

CHENIN BLANC
Flavors: Ripe apple, lemon drop, pear, honeydew
This wine is closely identified with Frances' Loire Valley, although it is grown around the world. It is arguably one of the least-appreciated great wine grape in the world, despite its tremendous versatility. Although it has many characteristics, depending on where it is grown, its ultimate expression comes out in slightly sweet wines. It is very versatile, and is grown everywhere.

GEWÜRZTRAMINER
Flavors: Lychee, grapefruit, flowers, talc
This grape reaches its apex in Alsace, where it produces intensely floral, aromatic, spicy wines ranging from bone dry to decadently sweet. In cooler climate regions such as Oregon and northern Italy (where it is called simply Traminer), it makes a crisp, grapefruity white wine that rarely sees oak and often pairs well with Asian dishes and spicy foods.

MARSANNE
Flavors: Marzipan, white peaches, pears
The most important white wine grape of the northern Rhône, Marsanne has only recently begun to be varietally labeled in the U.S. Both here and in France, it is often blended with Roussanne, Viognier, and (sometimes) Grenache Blanc. Marsanne ripens reliably and makes full-bodied, low-acid wines with flavors of almonds, white peaches, and lightly spiced pears. Australia boasts some of the oldest plantings in the world.

MUSCAT

Flavors: Oranges, tangerines

There are many varieties of Muscat throughout the world, but all are marked by a penetrating aroma of oranges. When fermented dry, Muscat's fruit-driven scents and flavors generally impart a hint of sweetness. It can be made into excellent light sparkling wines, especially the Moscato d'Asti of northern Italy, or rich dessert wines, such as Beaumes-de-Venise. The fortified Muscats of Australia take the grape to its most luscious and dense extremes.

PINOT BLANC

Flavors: Green apple, citrus

Similar to Chardonnay, but lighter and more elegant, Pinot Blanc has never acquired the cachet or reputation of its big brother Pinot Grigio. But in Alsace, northeast Italy, Oregon and parts of California some very nice versions are made, ranging from lightly herbal to spicy to citrusy. It's best when left in stainless steel; too much oak tends to change its innate characteristics.

PINOT GRIS/GRIGIO

Flavors: Citrus, fresh pear, melon

Pinot Grigio creates light, zippy, food-friendly white wines that don't clobber the palate with oak and alcohol. Most popular versions come from the Tre Venezie region of Italy, but Alsace and the Pfalz region of Germany also do well with the grape. Its alter ego, Pinot Gris (same grape, different name), has become the pre-eminent white wine of Oregon, where it produces lively, pear-flavored wines that may  carry a hint of fruity sweetness. The California versions are a bit heavier, but vintners in Washington make intense, tart wines that match well with seafood.

RIESLING

Flavors: Green apple, citrus, apricot, peach, honeysuckle

In flavor, Riesling ranges from dry and stony to floral and sweet, much like Chenin Blanc; and the sweetest versions can age for decades. The greatest Rieslings are the German wines of the Mosel-Saar-Ruwer, Rheinhessen, and Rheingau; close behind are those of Alsace.

Washington, New York, and Australia can lay claim to making the best examples of Riesling outside of Europe, from bone-dry Rieslings that marry beautifully with shellfish and Pacific Rim dishes, to sharply-etched, achingly-sweet late-harvest Rieslings and ice wines.

ROUSSANNE

Flavors: Lime, citrus, stone fruits
Roussanne is widely planted throughout southern France and has become quite popular among the "Rhône Rangers"—a group from California and Washington state dedicated to promoting Rhône varietals in America. Full-bodied and tasting of lime and citrus, its acids make Roussanne a fine blending partner for Marsanne.

SAUVIGNON/FUMÉ BLANC

Flavors: Grass, herb, citrus, pineapple, peach
Something of a chameleon grape that can deliver interesting flavors across a wide spectrum of ripeness, Sauvignon Blanc does well in widely diverse parts of the world. The Fumé Blanc moniker, coined in the 1970s by Robert Mondavi as a sales gimmick, is still commonly used and often indicates that the wine has been barrel-fermented. In Sancerre and Pouilly-Fumé in the Loire valley, it sports an aggressively herbaceous, grassy pungency, which combines with the bracing acids and stony minerality of the soils. It has become the benchmark white wine of New Zealand, where the intensity of the green citrus and berry fruit flavors is predominant. In California, it is made in a wide range of styles, but often ripened and barrel-fermented to taste like a peachy, tropical Chardonnay. Late-harvest Sauvignon Blanc, often blended with Sémillon, makes some of the greatest sweet wines in the world, most notably Sauternes.

SÉMILLON

Flavors: Fig, melon, light herb
Like Sauvignon Blanc, its frequent blending mate, Sémillon can make a fine, bone-dry white wine, notable for its texture and softly-grassy aromas, or it can be late-harvested, shriveled with botrytis, and turned into some of the world's greatest dessert wines. As a solo varietal, it has had sparse success, though Washington state does very well with the grape, as does Australia. Though

low in acid, Sémillons can age nicely and take on added layers of subtle spice and herb. Young Sémillons taste of figs and melons, adding leafy notes as they age.

VIOGNIER

Flavors: Flowers, citrus rind, apricot, peach

Viognier is intensely aromatic, and when perfectly ripened, smells of apricots, peaches, and citrus rind. It is a difficult wine to make, as it can be quite bitter and austere when not quite ripe, and turn flabby and hot when over-ripe. Excellent wines using this grape made in Washington, California, and Australia tend toward the ripe, hot, peachy styles. Viognier is also blended and/or co-fermented with Syrah, adding wonderful high notes of citrus and flower to the finished red wine.

Red Wine Grapes

CABERNET FRANC

Flavors: Violets, blueberry, earth, black olive, coffee

Along with Cabernet Sauvignon and Merlot, Cabernet Franc is part of the essential blending triad that makes up the majority of the Bordeaux blend (and Meritage) red wines produced in the United States. On its own, Cabernet Franc is a more tannic, earthy cousin to Cabernet Sauvignon. In warmer sites outside of Europe, its most distinctive attributes are its pure notes of violets and blueberry, and its ripe tannins often carry the scent of fresh-roasted coffee. It is made (though rarely labeled) as a varietal in Chinon, Bourgueil, and Saumur-Champigny, where it is hard and tannic and can evoke an austere minerality. In Pomerol and St-Emilion it is featured in blends with Merlot, adding a spicy, pungent, sometimes minty note.

CABERNET SAUVIGNON

Flavors: Bell pepper, green olive, herb, cassis, black cherry

The primary component of great Bordeaux and the defining grape of the Napa Valley, Cabernet Sauvignon is grown all over the world, but rarely achieves greatness. It ripens late and can be quite weedy and even vegetal in cooler climate regions such as Chile. In Bordeaux and Tuscany, it is almost always blended to soften its intensely astringent tannins. The Napa style is dense, purple-black, jammy, and tasting of currants and black cherries. Thick and ripe, layered with expensive new oak scents and flavors, it has found many admirers. In Washington,

the best Cabernet straddles the border between the ripeness of California versions and the nuanced herb, leaf, and olive flavors of great Bordeaux.

GAMAY
Flavors: Strawberry, raspberry, cherry
The grape of Beaujolais, Gamay is often made to be drunk quite young, and shows bright, tangy, fruit-driven flavors of strawberry, raspberry, and sweet cherries. When made by the method known as carbonic maceration (*see* Glossary), young Gamay has a slight effervescence and a distinct smell of bananas. Beaujolais Nouveau, released each year shortly after harvest, is the most famous example.

GRENACHE/GARNACHA
Flavors: Spice, cherry
Old vine Grenache makes some of the greatest red wines of both Spain and Australia, and is an important component of Châteauneuf-du-Pape, Gigondas, and Cotes-du-Rhône in France. An early-ripening grape, it tends toward high alcohol and low acidity. At its best it creates very fruity, spicy, bold-flavored wines somewhat reminiscent of a softer, less-intense version of Syrah.

MALBEC
Flavors: Sour cherry, spice
One of the less-prominent blending grapes of Bordeaux, Malbec has risen to prominence in Argentina, where it makes spicy, tart red wines that take well to aging in new oak barrels. Elsewhere it remains a minor player, though

a few varietally-labeled Malbecs are made in California and Washington.

MERLOT

Flavors: Watermelon, strawberry, cherry, plum

Merlot is the Chardonnay of reds, easy to pronounce, easy to like, agreeable, and versatile, but mostly lacking any substantive character of its own. The great exception is Chateau Pétrus, where it comprises ninety-five percent of the blend. Varietal Merlot rose to popularity in the 1990s but too many insipid, watery, over-priced Merlots took the bloom off the rose. Outside of Bordeaux, it is at its very best in Washington state, where it ripens beautifully and creates plump, powerful wines that can age for a decade or more.

MOURVÈDRE/MATARO

Flavors: Spice, cherry

This Mediterranean red grape is especially popular in France and Spain, making medium-bodied, lightly spicy wines with pretty, cherry-flavored fruit. The best sites also add a distinctive, gravelly minerality to the fruit. Some old vine plantings remain in California and also in Australia, where it is generally featured in a blend with Shiraz and Grenache.

NEBBIOLO

Flavors: Plum, pie cherry, tar

The principal grape of Barolo, Barbaresco, and Gattinara, Nebbiolo unquestionably belongs with the great red wines of the world, but has proven almost impossible to grow anywhere outside the Piedmont region of Italy. California versions, despite decades of effort, remain light, thin, and generic.

PINOT NOIR

Flavors: Tomato leaf, beet root, pale cherry, blackberry, cola, plum

Pinot Noir is the grape that winemakers love to hate; it is the prettiest, sexiest, most demanding, and least predictable of all. The template for great Pinot Noir is Burgundy, but even there the grape is flighty, fragile, and prone to obstinately weedy flavors. A principal component of many Champagnes and other sparkling wines, it can also be ripened to produce wines of surprising density and even jammyness in California, New Zealand, and warm sites in Oregon. Pinot Noir is best expressed as a pure varietal, and is often featured as a single-vineyard wine in Oregon and California, emulating the hundreds of tiny appellations of Burgundy. When at its best, Pinot has an ethereal delicacy yet can age for decades; it is most memorably described as "the iron fist in the velvet glove."

SANGIOVESE
Flavors: Pie cherry, anise, tobacco leaf
The principal grape of Tuscany, where it is the primary component of Chianti and Brunello di Montalcino. Sangiovese is relatively light in color and quite firmly acidic. In Italy, it shows distinctive flavors of pie cherry, anise, and tobacco; elsewhere it can be rather plain and undistinguished, though some promising bottles have come from Washington's Walla Walla Valley. Many of Italy's "Super Tuscan" (*see* Glossary) red blends marry Sangiovese to Cabernet Sauvignon, a combination that both strengthens the Sangiovese and smoothes out the Cabernet.

SYRAH/SHIRAZ
Flavors: Blackberry, boysenberry, plum, pepper, clove
Plantings of Syrah have exploded in California and Washington, where sappy, spicy, peppery, luscious versions are being made. Known as Shiraz in Australia, it is unarguably that country's claim to enological fame. Australian Shiraz is made in every conceivable style, from light and fruity to dense and tarry; it is made as a deep red, tannic sparkling wine, and also as a fortified "Port." In the northern Rhône, the most extraordinary expressions of the grape are produced, especially in Hermitage and Cote Rôtie, where its peppery, dense, spicy fruit is layered into unbelievably complex wines streaked with mineral, smoked meat, tar, wild herb, and leather.

ZINFANDEL
Flavors: Raspberry, blackberry, black cherry, raisin, prune
For decades, Zinfandel was California's grape, though now it is grown all over the west coast of the United States, in Australia, Italy, and elsewhere, and its ancestry has been traced to Croatia. But California Zinfandel remains the model for all others, and it grows well and vinifies distinctively all over the state. Mendocino makes somewhat rustic versions with hints of Asian spices; Dry Creek Zinfandels are racy and laden with raspberry. In certain areas of North and Central California it is hot, thick, and jammy, while in Napa it is plush with ripe, sweet black-cherry flavors. California Zinfandels now commonly reach 15 or 16 percent alcohol levels; sometimes even higher for late harvest versions. Zinfandel

Detail of a faucet on wine barrel.

"Ports" are also made. And of course the ever-popular White Zin blush wines remain a staple of sweet-wine connoisseurs and beginning wine drinkers.

Wine Terminology

Dry Most wines are dry. It simply means that the grapes were fermented until all the discernible sugar was converted to alcohol.

Crisp Indicates higher levels of acidity. Often used to describe white wines that have been fermented in stainless steel and given no exposure to new oak barrels.

Fruity Clean, fresh fruit flavors should be evident in young wines. As wines evolve, the fruit flavors may become dried or leathery. Fruit can give an impression of sweetness, even when a wine is dry.

Leesy Some white wines (Chardonnay and Pinot Gris, for example) are fermented in oak barrels and left the rest on the lees, which are, in part, the dead yeast cells. In the process they gain a certain creamy texture and complexity, but lose some fruitiness.

Oaky Vanilla, chocolate, toast, cedar, bacon fat and smoke are some of the flavors that may come from aging in new oak barrels. This well-loved range of flavors is often found in many Chardonnays and red wines.

Sweet Many inexpensive white wines are off-dry, which means they display a degree of sweetness. Dessert wines (such as ice wines, late harvests, fortifieds, etc.) are sweeter still.

Tannic A puckery sensation that comes from drinking or eating grapes or black tea. A dry, leafy astringency at the back of the tongue. More noticeable after drinking red wines.

CHAPTER FIVE

Where Wine Comes From

France

France is the source of some of the greatest wines in the world, but has also been the source of some of the worst. Despite a labeling system that is often confusing to many outside of France, French wine still gives the greatest pleasure of any wine-producing region. The style of French wine echoes that of the French themselves—elegant, well-dressed, showing an appreciation for the good things of life but never to excess. French wines go best with food, never overpowering either in flavor or in alcohol, always well-mannered, often beautiful.

The fact that, today, the quality of even the least-expensive French wine has improved impressively, means that there is a whole new range of wines open to wine drinkers.

All these qualities make it worthwhile to spend some time to get to know French wine and to appreciate its many facets. The country produces all styles of wine, from the cool wines of the Loire Valley, to the stylish whites of Alsace, through the classics of Bordeaux and Burgundy, to the more powerful, muscular offerings of the Rhône, to the warm wines of Languedoc and Roussillon, suffused with sun. And, of course, there are the great Champagnes.

Florimont vineyard in France.

In a world of international brands, where origin doesn't matter, France offers an alternative ethos. There is much talk of *terroir*, of the place and the culture from which a wine comes. It makes every wine different, makes many of them special. There is no homogeneity here.

France is an ordered country, and despite the seeming chaos of French wine, there is order in the system. Wines come from places, and these places are designated appellations. An appellation—*appellation contrôlée* on a wine label—is not a guarantee of quality. It is a guarantee of origin, and a guarantee that the wine has been made following certain rules specifying grape varieties, soil, planting, yields, and winemaking. The wine has also passed a sensory test which approves its style and its typicity for the appellation.

There are nearly 280 appellations in France, ranging from the huge—Bordeaux appellation, or Champagne—to the tiny, single-vineyard appellations of Coulée de Serrant in the Loire Valley and Romanée-Conti in Burgundy. There are regional appellations, there are district appellations, and there are appellations which cover only one commune.

A good example of this hierarchy is in Burgundy. The main appellation of the region is plain and simple: red and white, Bourgogne Rouge or Bourgogne Blanc. Climbing up the hierarchy are district appellations such as Chablis, for white wines, Mâcon for white and red wines, Côte de Beaune for reds, and so on.

Rising again in quality while the area of the appellation gets smaller are village appellations: Vougeot, Auxey-Duresse, Pommard, Nuits-St-Georges. In these villages, certain superior vineyards are designated *premier cru*—and you will find the name of the vineyard on the label. At the top of the quality heap are the single-vineyard appellations, the Grand Cru: Clos de Vougeot being perhaps the most famous.

There is one other category of wine which is in some ways the most interesting and exciting: Vin de Pays. These are everyday, ready-to-drink wines that offer some of the best values in the world. The labels, unlike appellation wines, will show grape varieties. Coming generally from the warm south of France, the wines will be warm, ripe, and fruity. The best-known example is Vin de Pays d'Oc.

Having established some of the ground rules for French wine, let's examine the fascinations of the different regions in more detail.

By far the largest, the most important, and one of the best regions, both for great wines and for bargains, is Bordeaux. Great reds from the great chateaus are what make the headlines, but Bordeaux is so big, that there is plenty of choice. Appellations with the name *Côtes* in the title are always worth seeking out, as are the white wines (yes, Bordeaux makes whites, both dry and sweet). And the general level of quality has improved dramatically. The reds are fruity, but never over-alcoholic, always with a layer of tannin that makes them great food wines. The whites are fresh, the best with wood flavors to give complexity. They may all be called "chateau this," "chateau that," but that's simply a way of saying that many Bordeaux wines come from one individual property.

Cabernet Sauvignon, Merlot, and Cabernet Franc are the main red grapes; Sauvignon Blanc and Sémillon are the main whites. But most Bordeaux is not a single varietal wine—it is more often a blend, which makes these wines more than the sum of their individual parts.

Burgundy is the other big French wine. It is a fifth the size of the Bordeaux region, and produces correspondingly more expensive wines, with fewer bargains, and more disappointments. The best way to buy Burgundy is to follow the best producers, and reliable reviews from buying guides or wine magazines. If you take that advice, the most seductive wines (red from Pinot Noir, white from Chardonnay, always 100 percent) are in your glass. It's not just chance that the Burgundy bottle has rounded sides, the Bordeaux bottle has straight: Burgundy appeals to the senses, Bordeaux to the intellect.

Much larger in scale than Burgundy is the Rhône valley. From the alcoholic and powerful highs of Châteauneuf-du-Pape, through the dense elegance of the Syrah wines of appellations like Côte-Rôtie and Hermitage, this is red wine country. Rich and generous, these wines appeal to wine drinkers used to California reds. And, just like Bordeaux, there is also great value to be found in this region: wines labeled Côtes du Rhône. If they have a village name attached (Rasteau and Seguret are among the best), they will be that much better, even if more expensive.

Bordeaux, Burgundy, and the Rhône are the best-known wine regions of France except for Champagne. This sparkling wine from the chalk slopes east of Paris is France's best answer to a global brand. It is the drink of celebration, of success, and the best way to drown sorrows. And, unlike the still French wines, which have been successfully copied around the world, Champagne remains inimitable, despite thousands of attempts. The combination of cool climate, chalk soil and—there's no other word for it—terroir are just so special.

As a complete contrast, there are the hot, sun-drenched vineyards of the south. Languedoc and Roussillon don't just produce tanker loads of inexpensive wine. Some areas such as Corbières, Minervois, Coteaux du Languedoc, and Côtes de Roussillon offer a magic mix of great value, history, and some fascinating herbal and fruity flavors.

After these greats, come the Loire and Alsace regions, which produce some of the greatest and most fascinating wines in France. Bordeaux and the Rhône are known for reds, Burgundy for reds and whites. The two cool-climate areas of Loire and Alsace are where the whites shine.

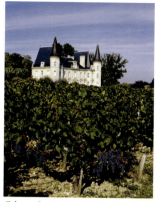

Cabernet Sauvignon grapes in a vineyard at Château Pichon-Longueville-Baron, Pauillac, Gironde, France.

Alsace is unique in France in that producers are allowed to put the grape variety on the label of an appellation wine. It is also unique in that the grapes are a mix of German and French: Riesling and Gewürztraminer, Muscat and Pinot Gris. These are not light wines, but they have a fruitiness and a richness that is quite different from the German models just across the Rhine river. At the top of this list are the Alsace Grand Cru vineyards, single vineyards that can produce astonishing quality and longevity.

The Loire Valley is a complete mix. Every style of wine can be found along its six-hundred-mile length. The greatest styles are the Sauvignon Blanc of Sancerre and Pouilly-Fume, the models for Sauvignon Blanc around the world. And the Chenin Blancs of the central Loire—the sweet wines of Vouvray and Anjou—have a poise and acidity which allows them to age for decades, yet be fresh when young. The dry Chenins of Savennières are the purest expression of their granite soil to be found. Finally, to complete the mix are the reds of Chinon and Bourgueil and the fresh, easy whites of Muscadet.

It's obvious from this brief list that France has variety, in profusion perhaps, but it does mean that there is never a dull moment when reaching for a bottle of French wine. If your wish is to have the same, safe bottle of wine every day, then non-European brands are the better option.

Italy

In ancient times, the Italian peninsula was commonly referred to as *enotria*, or "land of wine," because of its rich diversity of grape varieties and many acres dedicated to cultivated vines. In more ways than one, Italy became a gigantic nursery and a commercial hub fortuitously positioned at the heart of the Mediterranean for what would become

Tenuta la Volta, near Barolo, Piemonte, Italy.

western civilization's first "globally" traded product: wine.

Italy's prominence in the global wine industry has in no way diminished despite millennia of history. The sun-drenched North-South peninsula that extends from the thirty-sixth to the forty-sixth parallel embodies pockets of geographical, geological, and climatic perfection between the Upper Adige and the island of Pantelleria for the production of quality wine. Italian tradition is so closely grafted to the vine that the good cheer and easy attitudes associated with wine culture are mirrored in the nation's temperament.

Despite Italy's long affinity with *vitis vinifera*, the Italian wine industry has experienced an invigorating rebirth over the past three decades that truly sets it apart from other European wine nations. American baby boomers may still recall watery Valpolicella or Chianti Classico in hay-wrapped flasks at neighborhood New York eateries, or the generic "white" and "red" wines of Sicily's Corvo. Wines like those cemented Italy's reputation as a quantity (as opposed to quality, like in France) producer of wines sold at attractive prices. But as Italy gained confidence during the prosperous post-war years in the areas of design, fashion, and gastronomy, it demonstrated renewed attention to wine. Thanks to a small band of primarily Tuscan vintners, Italy launched itself with aggressive determination onto the world stage as a producer of some of the best wines ever produced anywhere: Amarone, Barolo, Brunello di Montalcino, and Passito di Pantelleria.

Like a happy epidemic, modern viticulture and enological techniques swept across the Italian peninsula throughout the 1980s and 1990s: Vertical shoot positioning and bilateral cordon trellising in vineyards; stainless steel, temperature-controlled fermentation, and *barrique* wood aging in wineries. As profits soared, producers reinvested in technology, personnel, and high-priced consultants, and a modern Italian wine revolution had suddenly taken place.

As it stands, Italy is the world's second-largest producer of wine after France. Each year, one in fifty Italians is involved with the grape harvest. And like France, Italy has adopted a rigorously controlled appellation system that imposes strict controls, with regulations governing vineyard quality, yields per acre, and aging practices among other things. There are over three hundred DOC (*Denominazioni di Origine Controllata*) and DOCG (*Denominazioni di Origine Controllata e Garantita)* wines today, and the classifications increase to over five hundred when IGT (*Indicazioni Geografica Tipica*) wines are factored in. Thanks to this system, Italy's fifty thousand wineries enjoy a competitive advantage when it comes to the production and sales of quality wines.

Interestingly, there is a second wine revolution underway that promises to unlock potential uniquely associated with Italy. It is the re-evaluation and celebration of Italy's rich patrimony of "indigenous" grapes. (Because some varieties actually originated outside Italy, producers often refer to them as "traditional" varieties instead.) These are grapes—like Nero d'Avola, Fiano, Sagrantino, and Teroldego—that only modern *enotria* can offer to world consumers. As a result, a rapidly increasing number of vintners from Italy's twenty winemaking regions are banking on "traditional" varieties to distinguish themselves in a market dominated by "international" varieties, such as Merlot, Cabernet Sauvignon, and Chardonnay.

NORTH

The Italian Alps butt against the long expanses of the Po River plains leaving tiny pockets and microclimates along the foot of the mountains that are each linked to their own special wine. Starting in northwestern Piedmont, Nebbiolo grapes form two tall pillars of Italy's wine legacy: Barolo and Barbaresco, named in the French tradition after the hilltop hamlets where the wines were born. Like in Burgundy, the exclusivity of these wines has a lot to do with the winemakers' battle against nature and the wine's extraordinary ability to age. Rare vintages like the stellar 1985 or 1990 Barolos are the darlings of serious wine collectors.

Further east, in the Veneto region, vintners follow an ancient formula in which wine is made from raisins dried on straw mats. With its higher concentration and alcohol, silky Amarone is Italy's most distinctive wine and can command record prices for new releases. The Veneto,

Trentino, Alto Adige, and Friuli-Venezia Giulia are celebrated for their white wines—such as the phenomenally successful Pinot Grigio. Italy's best sparkling wine is made in Trentino and the Franciacorta area of Lombardy (known as the "Champagne of Italy") under strict regulation with Pinot Noir and Chardonnay grapes.

CENTER

With its cypress-crested hills and beautiful stone farmhouses, Tuscany is the pin-up queen of Italian enology. The region's iconic dreamscape has helped promote the image of Italian wine abroad like no other. Within Tuscany's borders is a treasure-trove of excellent wines: Chianti Classico, Brunello di Montalcino, Vino Nobile di Montepulciano, San Gimignano whites, Bolgheri and Maremma reds. Italy's wine revolution started here when storied producers like Piero Antinori worked outside appellation regulations to make wines blended with international varieties such as Cabernet Sauvignon. These wines are known as Super Tuscans and are considered on par with the top *crus* of Bordeaux and California.

Central Italy delivers many more exciting wines, such as Sagrantino from the Umbrian town of Montefalco, dense and dark Montepulciano from Abruzzo, and white Verdicchio from Le Marche.

SOUTH AND ISLANDS

The regions of southern Italy, and the island of Sicily in particular, are regarded as Italy's enological frontier: Relaxed regulation and increased experimentation promise a bright future for vintners and investors alike. In many ways, Italy's south is a "new world" wine region locked within the confines of an "old world" wine reality. This unique duality has many betting on its enological promise.

Campania boasts wonderful whites, such as Fiano and Greco di Tufo that embody crisp, mineral characteristics from volcanic soils. Its red is Taurasi ("the Barolo of the south"), made from Aglianico. That same grape makes Basilicata's much-hyped Aglianico del Vulture. Puglia, the "heel" of the boot of Italy, was mostly a producer of bulk wine, but holds it own today among nascent wine regions with its powerhouse Primitivo and Negroamaro grapes.

Sicily has shown keen marketing savvy in bringing media attention to its native grapes like Nero d'Avola (red) and Grillo (a white once used in the production of fortified wine Marsala) and has done a great job of promoting the south of Italy in general. Some of Europe's most sensuous dessert wines, like the honey-rich Passito di Pantelleria, come from Sicily's satellite islands. The Mediterranean's other big island, Sardinia, is steadily working on its Cannonau and Vermentino grapes to raise the bar on quality there.

Germany

German wine labels can be intimidating: long foreign words and ornate gothic script are enough to make many consumers head for a different section of the wine shop. But for the initiated—and you'll qualify after reading this quick primer—German wine labels are among the most descriptive out there.

Harvesting Riesling grapes in the Pettenthal vineyard, Nackenheim, Germany.

As on any wine label, you'll find the name of the producer, the vintage, the region, and sometimes the name of the grape.

In addition to the grape-growing region (see below), most labels will show the names of the town and the vineyard in large type, such as *Graacher Himmelreich* (the town of Graach, Himmelreich vineyard). In much smaller type will be the terms *Qualitätswein bestimmter Anbaugebiete* (often just Qualitätswein, or QbA), indicating a "quality wine," or *Qualitätswein mit Prädikat* (QmP), denoting a quality wine picked at designated minimum ripeness levels that vary by grape variety and growing region. These ripeness levels will be indicated on the label as follows:

Kabinett The least ripe of the prädikat levels, and typically the lightest of a grower's offerings. With their low alcohol levels and touch of sweetness, these wines make ideal picnic quaffs and mouth-watering apéritifs. Most often consumed in their youth, they can last for ten years or more.

Spätlese Literally, "late picked." These grapes are generally only late-picked with respect to those grapes that go into Kabinett or QbA wines. If vinified dry (an increasingly popular style), they can still seem less than optimally ripe. Traditionally made, with some residual sugar left in, they are extremely food friendly. Try them with anything from Asian food to baked ham and roast fowl. Most should be consumed before age twenty.

Label on a bottle of Zimmermann-Graeff.

Auslese Made from "select" bunches of grapes left on the vine until they achieve high sugar readings, these wines often carry a hint or more of botrytis (*see* Glossary). While some are sweet enough to serve with simple fruit desserts, others are best sipped alone. With age, some of the sugar seems to melt away, yielding wines that can ably partner with roast pork or goose. Thirty-year-old auslesen can smell heavenly, but sometimes fall flat on the palate. Enjoy them on release for their luscious sweet fruit, or cellar for ten to twenty years.

Beerenauslese "Berry select" wines are harvested berry by berry, taking only botrytis-affected fruit. While auslesen are usually sweet, this level of ripeness elevates the wine to the dessert-only category. Hold up to fifty years.

Trockenbeerenauslese These "dried berry select" wines are made from individually harvested, shriveled grapes that have been heavily affected by botrytis. Profoundly sweet and honeyed, their over-the-top viscosity and sweetness can turn off some tasters, while others revel in the complex aromas and flavors.

Eiswein Made from frozen grapes that are at least equivalent in sugar levels to beerenauslese, but which produce wines with much racier levels of acidity. The intense sugars and acids enable these wines to easily endure for decades.

Aside from the ripeness levels denoted by the QmP system, you can expect to see the terms *trocken* and *halbtrocken* on some labels (their use is optional). Trocken, or dry, may be used on wines with fewer than 9g/L residual sugar (less than 0.9 percent); halbtrocken (half-dry) refers to wines with between 9 and 18g/L. Given the allowable ranges, these wines may be truly dry or verging on sweet, depending on acid-sugar balance.

In an effort to simplify German labels, a few relatively new terms have cropped up that supplement, replace, or partially replace the traditional labeling system. *Erstes Gewächs* wines, or "first growths," come only from designated sites in the Rheingau. Classic wines must be "harmoniously dry" and must omit references to specific villages or vineyards. Selection wines bear a single-vineyard designation on the label and must be dry.

GERMAN WINE REGIONS

Most of the classic German wine regions are closely identified with river valleys, the slopes of which provide the proper exposure for ripening grapes at this northern latitude. Virtually all of Germany's best wines come from the Riesling grape, but there are several exceptions, like the fine Gewürztraminers from Fitz-Ritter in the Pfalz and Valckenberg in Rheinhessen and the exquisite Rieslaners and Scheurebes from Müller-Catoir in the Pfalz.

Mosel-Saar-Ruwer The coolest of the German growing regions, and home to Germany's crispest, raciest, and most delicate Rieslings. Green apples, floral notes, and citrus are all likely descriptors, but the best wines also display fine mineral notes that express their slate-driven terroirs.

Rheingau Steep slate slopes and slightly warmer temperatures than found in the Mosel-Saar-Ruwer yield powerful, sturdy wines, with ripe fruit flavors underscored by deep minerality.

Rheinhessen Source for much of Germany's production, quality here can vary from generic liebfraumilch to fine single-estate wines.

Nahe This small side valley is the only rival to the Mosel-Saar-Ruwer for elegance and finesse, with Rieslings that balance lightness of body with mineral-based tensile strength.

Pfalz One of Germany's warmest winegrowing regions, with a great diversity of soils, microclimates, and grape varieties. Dry styles, whether made from Riesling or other white grapes, are more common here, and show better balance than those from cooler regions. Spätburgunder (Pinot Noir) is also more successful here than elsewhere.

Wines from other German winegrowing regions, such as the Ahr, Baden, Franken, and Württemberg are infrequently seen in the United States.

Austria

Thanks to two grapes, and two wine styles, Austrian wine has an important presence on the international wine-making stage. One of these grapes is Riesling, of which Austrian wine producers are some of the greatest exponents. The other is Grüner Veltliner, of which Austrian wine producers have a virtual monopoly, but one they exploit with panache and stunning results.

The wine styles are both white, but otherwise completely different. There are beautifully crisp, balanced, dry whites; and there are some of the most impressive sweet, botrytis wines, rich, unctuous, and intense.

Austrian vineyards at Retz, Niederösterreich.

These are the traditional Austrian wine styles. In recent years, red wines have become increasingly important and of better quality. Using local as well as international grape varieties, Austrian reds now cover one third of the country's vineyards.

Austria's wine-making history goes back to ancient Roman days, with some of today's best vineyards planted at that time, Grape varieties—red and white—are found on Austrian labels, along with the geographic origin. Today's Austrian vineyards are found in the east of country, whereas classic areas are along the Danube Valley, north-west of Vienna, and in the far east in the province of Burgenland.

The Danube Valley offers superlatives, both in wine and in wine country. The beautiful Wachau vineyards, best known but also one of the smallest wine regions, are caught between steep mountain slopes and the wide

Danube River. The purest, most elegant Rieslings and Grüner Veltliners are made by a succession of some of the best producers in Austria. Quality levels are specific to the region: the lightest style is Steinfelder, next is Ferderspiel, and the richest style is Smaragd.

Other Danube districts include the Kremstal and Kamptal. Both make great white wines: the Kamptal produces some of the most characteristic Gruner Veltliner, crisp, dry, and peppery, from vineyards that are generally cooler than those of Kremstal. One of Austria's most famed vineyard sites, Heiligenstein (rock of saints), is in Kremstal.

North of the Danube, stretching away to the northeast corner of the country, is the Weinviertel, the largest Austrian wine area. Great value wines come from here, mainly made with Grüner Veltliner. A new wine designation is DAC, modeled on the French AC or the Italian DOC: stressing geographic origin rather than grape variety, DAC wines are some of the best everyday dry white wines coming out of Austria.

The Burgenland is where the great dessert wines, and—increasingly—red wines come from. This is the hottest region of Austria, dominated by the marshy, shallow Neusiedlersee lake. Great sweet wines come from the villages all around the lake, while reds come from here as well as hillier vineyards further south.

Wines from Styria, a smaller area in the south east, are worth seeking out. The region has astonished the world with the quality of its Sauvignon Blanc and Chardonnay, and some great white wine makers are based there, as well.

Spain

Among European countries with long winemaking histories, no country has come further in recent years than Spain. As the nation with more acreage under vine than any of its continental mates, Spain is no longer simply a producer of overcropped, basic wines destined for domestic consumption. Just the opposite: in less than two decades, Spain has evolved into one of Europe's most exciting and progressive wine producers.

Today Spanish winemakers are making sought-after wines at almost every price point and quality level, and in most of the country's sixty-plus denominated regions. From everyday reds made from grapes including Tempranillo, Monastrell, and Garnacha, to crisp whites like Albariño and Verdejo, to frothy Cava and some of the world's finest and richest red and dessert wines, Spain is offering the consumer variety and value at almost every turn.

Harvesting Xarel-lo grapes in a vineyard at Cavas Chandon, the Spanish branch of Moët et Chandon.

Talk about a 180-degree turnabout; twenty years ago, nobody thought much of Spain's wines. In those early post-Franco years, the country featured one collectable red—the idiosyncratic and esoteric Vega Sicilia (still one of the world's great red wines). Meanwhile, Rioja boasted a few highly traditional wines (read: not that fruity, with a lot of American oak flavor) in López de Heredia's Viña Tondonia, Marqués de Riscal, and CUNE, among others. Beyond that, there wasn't much to talk about besides Torres' Sangre de Toro and the dry and sweet fortified wines coming from Jerez in the south.

By the middle of the 1990s and into the twenty-first century, however, the world's thirst for better, more distinctive wines gave Spain the necessary spur in the side that it needed to push the envelope. Younger winemakers, many trained outside the country, started to replace their more traditional predecessors. Older regions that had fallen out of style were invigorated with new plantings and the construction of modern wineries. And almost before you could say *Olé*, quality wines were emerging from all four corners of the country and quite a few places in between.

SPAIN'S WINES AND REGIONS

There are currently more than sixty regulated wine regions in Spain. The most prominent *denominaciones de origen*, as the regions are called, have been around for decades if not longer; places like Rioja, Ribera Del Duero, Jerez, Rias Baixas, Priorat, Penedès, Navarra, La Mancha, and Valdepeñas. Others have risen to prominence during the aforementioned growth boom: Rueda, Bierzo, Toro, Cigales, Somontano, Yecla, Jumilla, and Montsant, while not all young, fit the mold of up and coming. And there are still a few DOs that seem stuck in time; outposts like Extremadura, located along the border with Portugal, and Utiel-Requena (inland from Valencia) that may have their day down the line.

Among red-wine regions, the spotlight is shining brightest on Rioja, Ribera Del Duero, Priorat and, to a lesser degree, Toro and Bierzo. Rioja is one of Spain's larger DOs, and the focus here is on Tempranillo. Rioja came to prominence in the 1800s when French winemakers fled their country's phylloxera *(see* Glossary) epidemic, and over time three main styles of red wine have evolved: *crianzas*, which are wood-aged wines generally of lighter stature; *reservas*, which spend extended time in barrel; and *gran reserva*, theoretically the ripest and most age-worthy of wines. Look for modern, extracted, flavorful wines from the likes of Allende, LAN, Muga, Remelluri, Remírez de Ganuza, Roda, and a host of other newcomers. Marqués de Murrieta, Marqués de Cáceres, Montecillo, and the previously mentioned CUNE and Riscal comprise the respected old guard.

Ribera Del Duero, Toro, Cigales, and other sections of Castilla y León province are also prime Tempranillo areas. Modern wineries like Alion, Pingus, Viña Sastre, and others in Ribera, as well as Numanthia-Termes in Toro are the new-wave leaders, while Vega Sicilia, Pesquera, Protos, and Pérez Pascuas have been plying their trade in Ribera for longer, with commendable results.

Just to the southwest of Barcelona lies Penedès, the heart of Spain's sparkling wine industry. Here wineries harvest the white grapes Macabeo, Parellada, and Xarello before blending them into what's known as Cava. This sparkling wine is made similarly to Champagne but is lighter and far less complex than France's prized bubbly. Penedès is also home to Miguel Torres S.A., one of Spain's preeminent wineries, a survivor of the Spanish Civil War, and for many years when Spain was overlooked, a major exporter to the United States.

A little further southwest of Penedès are Priorat and Montsant, regions that can trace their winemaking roots back to the Romans and later Carthusian monks. Here Garnacha and old Cariñena vines yield powerful wines, and the current crop of winemakers is, almost to a person, young, ambitious, and iconoclastic. Today Priorat is producing some of the world's finest red wines, ones that compare with the best of France, Italy, and California.

Lastly, Sherry is the fortified sipper of Andalusia. From crisp fino and manzanilla up to richer, nuttier amontillado and oloroso, Sherry is a unique wine for either before a meal or after. Sherry predates Spain's vinous renaissance by centuries, but never has it gone out of style.

Portugal

Portugal has always had Port. Vintage Port and Late Bottled Vintage Port are the best sellers in the United States, but aged tawnies should command increasing interest. With the great strides in winemaking techniques and the results of great research into grape varieties and vineyard sites being put into practice, Portugal's Port is entering a golden age.

What makes Portugal so exciting at the moment is that the same can now be said of Portuguese table wines. The days of Portugal being known for only lightly sparkling Rosé are long gone, although the wines themselves are still widely available. Increasingly, wines with the quality to be poured at the top international tables are arriving in America from Portugal, and the number of these wines is increasing with each new harvest.

Encouragingly, Portugal has not copied the rest of the world. As with the Italians, Portuguese winemakers have not capitulated to international grape varieties and tastes. But, unlike the Italians, who enjoy playing with Cabernet, Chardonnay, and have acres of Merlot, Portuguese vineyards are still almost entirely planted with the great native varietals.

The boiler house of new developments in Portugal is the Douro Valley. Many of the same people who also make Port are making the greatest table wines. They use Portugal's greatest red grape varieties, Touriga Nacional, Tinta Roriz, Tinta Franca, Souzão, Tinta Cão, and Tinta Barroca, generally blended, invariably wood aged (although often in large wood barrels). The tastes are powerful, intense, tannic; the wines are long-lived.

South of the Douro, the Dão region also makes reds, which can be ageworthy (see Glossary). The Dão, lacking the same wealth of winemaking talent, has lagged behind, but there are now enough producers of quality to show that the style of the reds is going to be less intense than the Douro, more mineral, more herbal.

But Portugal is not only a red wine country. One of the country's most famous wines, Vinho Verde, produced in the far north of the country, is normally seen overseas in its white version (the tart, acid red stays at home and is drunk with sardines). At its best, Vinho Verde can equal some of the whites of the Rias Baixas region of Spain.

More southerly regions of Portugal bring us back to red wine. The Alentejo, the Ribatejo, and Estremadura are three vineyards that straddle the center of the country. These are the good value areas, which can often reach fascinating heights of quality. Warmer and softer wines than the tannic giants of the Douro are produced in greater quantities, making these regions the best way of starting into the adventure of today's Portuguese wines.

California

California wines account for a sisty-four percent share of the United States wine market, according to the Wine Institute, the venerable trade and lobbying group whose membership includes 840 wineries. However, *Wine Business Monthly*, a trade magazine, estimates that there are 2,445 wineries doing business in California.

Vineyard on the western slopes of the Napa Valley, Oakville, Napa County, California.

Whatever the number, in 2004 California wineries produced wine grown on 440,296 acres of vineyards, about sixty percent of them planted with red or black grapes. The most widely planted major varietals, not surprisingly, are Chardonnay and Cabernet Sauvignon, although the latter has seen a slight percentage drop in recent years, as more Syrah and Pinot Noir have been planted.

The Central Valley of California contains the majority of plantings, but grapes from this hot inland region are seldom if ever included in premium bottlings. California's reputation for world-class wine rests almost entirely on coastal bottlings, "coastal" being defined as anywhere a true maritime influence penetrates the land, through gaps in the Coast Ranges that run from Oregon down to below Los Angeles. The Pacific Ocean is a chilly body of water, even in high summer. Without the gaps, California's coastal valleys would be almost as hot as the Central Valley, and incapable of producing fine, dry table wine. With the gaps, however, come the cooling winds and fogs that make for premium grape growing.

PREDOMINANT VARIETIES

Cabernet Sauvignon The great grape of the Médoc, in France's Bordeaux region, which has been the model—and point of departure—for California claret-style wines for more than a century.

Napa County dominates statewide acreage of Cabernet, as well as quality. The great estates of Napa Valley have been joined by scores of small, ambitious boutique wineries on the cutting edge of viticultural and enological—and pricing—practices. California Cabernet is rich, full-bodied, opulent, fruity, and hedonistic, matching supreme power with a velvety elegance. The best will easily age for a decade or two.

Pinot Noir Undoubtedly the great varietal success story of the late twentieth century in California wine, red or white, Pinot Noir continues to make the most astounding advances. It favors the coolest climates available, although if growing conditions are too chilly, the grapes fail to ripen. Pinot Noir is far more demanding to grow than almost any other wine grape, but when conditions are right, the wines can be majestic: lush, silky, complex, and (to use an overworked but useful word) seductive.

Chardonnay For at least fifty years, Chardonnay has been California's greatest dry white wine. Although in the 1990s the media touted an "A.B.C." phenomenon—anything but Chardonnay—the wine remains a triumph. Like Pinot Noir, Chardonnay is best grown in cool coastal conditions, although it is more forgiving, and the odd bottling from anywhere can gain praise. Full-throttle Burgundian winemaking is the norm, but lately, Australian-style unoaked Chardonnay has been enjoying favor.

Zinfandel Historians still quibble about when exactly this varietal came to California. It has been here for at least one-hundred-and-fifty years, and always has had its admirers. Zinfandel comes into and goes out of fashion, and has been made in styles ranging from sweet and Porty to dry and tannic to "white." The current thinking leans toward balance, in the model of a good Cabernet. The best Zinfandels come from cool coastal regions, especially old vines, most usually in Sonoma and Napa, but the Sierra Foothills have many old vineyards that produce great bottlings. Paso Robles occasionally comes up with a masterpiece.

Sauvignon Blanc This great grape of Sancerre and Pouilly-Fumé, in the Loire Valley, similarly produces a dry,

Benziger vineyards in the Sonoma Mountains west of Glen Ellen, Sonoma County, California.

crisp, pleasantly clean wine in California. It can be tank fermented and entirely unoaked, or just slightly oaked, in order to preserve the variety's fresh, citrusy flavors. Some producers look to Bordeaux to craft richer, barrel-fermented wines, often mixed with Sémillon, or even Viognier. "Fumé" Blanc is a synonym. If overcropped or unripe, the wines can have unpleasant aromas.

Merlot This other great grape of Bordeaux was greeted with fanfare by critics in the 1980s and 1990s, but Merlot never really reached Cabernet's superstardom. Merlot was said to be the "soft" Cabernet, but with modern tannin management, it's no softer than Cabernet, and, in fact can be quite hard. The wines, though, can be exceptional, especially in Napa Valley, Carneros, and parts of Sonoma County and Santa Barbara.

SYRAH AND RHÔNE VARIETIES

Plantings of Syrah have increased, as consumers and critics alike welcome these deeply fruity, richly balanced wines. Syrah grapes are remarkably adaptable, and grow well almost everywhere. The wines tend to be organized into cool-climate and warm-climate bottlings, the former drier and more tannic, the latter often soft and jammy. The other red Rhône varieties, especially Mourvèdre and Grenache, are still exotic specimens, tinkered with lovingly by a coterie of Rhône Rangers.

OTHER DRY WHITES

Voignier, the darling of the Northern Rhône, grew in popularity in the 1990s. The wine achieved fame for its exotic, full-throttle fruit, floral, and spice flavors, but proved surprisingly elusive when it came to balance. An emerging handful display true Alsatian richness and complexity. The best are from cool coastal valleys, but if the climate is too cold, the wines turn acidic and green.

MAJOR CALIFORNIA WINE REGIONS

American grape-growing regions are authorized by the federal government, upon petitioning from individuals, and are called "American Viticultural Areas" (AVAs), or "appellations." Currently, there are ninety-five AVAs in California, with more petitions filed everyday.

Napa Valley The state's oldest AVA is its most famous. Napa Valley (established in 1981), at 225,000 acres, is so large that over the years, it has developed fourteen appellations within the larger one. Napa always has been home to California's, and America's, greatest Cabernet Sauvignons and blends, an achievement not likely to be upset anytime soon. In all other varieties, it strives, usually successfully, to compete.

Sonoma County Sonoma is California's most heterogeneous wine county. So diverse is its climate, from hot and sunny inland to cool, foggy coastal, that every grape varietal in the state is grown somewhere within its borders, often as not to good effect. In warm Alexander Valley and Dry Creek Valley, Zinfandel finds few peers. Out on the coast, and the adjacent Russian River Valley, Pinot Noir first proved that California could compete with Burgundy, and Pinot's huge improvements continue to startle. Chardonnay excels everywhere; Syrah is dependable. Old-vine field blends, comprised often of obscure French varieties, have their admirers. Meanwhile, Alexander Valley Cabernet, especially from the steep, rugged west-facing slopes of the Mayacamas Mountains, is showing continuing improvement.

Monterey County This large, cool growing area originally was planted with huge vineyards, making inexpensive wine in industrial-sized quantities. Serious, boutique-oriented adventurers sought out nooks and crannies where they could produce world-class wine, and the Santa Lucia Highlands AVA (1992) has been the most noteworthy result. Its slopes and benches are home to ripe, full-bodied, high-acid Pinot Noir, Chardonnay and, increasingly, Syrah.

San Luis Obispo County Sandwiched between Monterey to the north and Santa Barbara to the south, this coastal county often is overlooked. But its twin AVAs, Edna Valley and Arroyo Grande Valley, arguably produce some of California's most distinguished Pinots and Chardonnays. A few vintners have made enormous strides with cool-climate Syrah and other Rhône varieties.

Santa Barbara County If any county deserves the honor for greatest achievements in winemaking over the last twenty years, it is this South-Central Coast region. The action began in the inland Santa Ynez Valley, a warmish-to-hot AVA. Years of experiments have shown the valley's aptitude for lush, complex red Rhône wines and Sauvignon Blanc. Merlot has been an unexpected star; Cabernet Sauvignon has not yet shown greatness. Closer to the ocean, the newest AVA, Santa Rita Hills (2001), was on critics' radar for Pinot Noir for showing lush fruit with an acidity found in few other regions. Chardonnay follows the same pattern. As in most cool-climate growing areas, determined wine makers tinker with Syrah, often excitingly.

Mendocino County Inland Mendocino is hot and mountainous. Beyond an individual winery here and there, it has yet to make a name for itself. The county's cool AVA is Anderson Valley, which has shown great promise in Pinot Noir.

The Sierra Foothills This enormous, multi-county region sprawls along the foothills of the Sierra Nevada Mountains. At their best, Foothills wines can be varietally pure, with Zinfandel taking the lead, although Cabernet Franc has been an unexpected star. Too many Foothills vintners, unfortunately, produce wines whose rusticity and high alcohol outweigh their charm.

Washington

In barely three decades, the Washington wine industry has risen from a half-dozen wineries trying their hand at a bit of Riesling, Gewürztraminer, and experimental plots of Pinot Noir and Cabernet, to become a global player. The state now boasts more than 375 wineries, 30,000 vineyard acres, and a track record for producing crisply etched, vibrantly fruity Rieslings; sleek and polished Chardonnays; ripe and flavorful Sémillons; bold, luscious Merlots; well-defined, muscular Cabernets; and vivid, smoky, saturated Syrahs.

Mount Rainier viewed over vineyards near Zillah, Washington.

Though a distant second to California in terms of total production, Washington wines get more medals and higher scores and sell for lower average prices on a percentage basis. There are seven appellations, all but one (the Puget Sound AVA) lying east of the Cascade mountains. The largest AVA by far is the Columbia Valley, a vast area of scrubby desert, punctuated by irrigated stretches of farmland with row crops, hops, orchards, and vineyards. The Cascade Mountains protect this inland desert from the cool, wet maritime climate of western Washington. Eastern Washington summers are hot and dry, and during the growing season, the vines average two extra hours of sunlight per day.

Inside the Columbia Valley AVA are the smaller appellations of Yakima Valley, Walla Walla Valley, Red Mountain, and Horse Heaven Hills. A sixth, the Columbia Gorge AVA, lies just to the west along the Columbia river.

Several factors account for Washington's unique wine-growing profile. Its vines are planted on their own roots, as phylloxera (*see* Glossary) has not been a problem in the state. Most vineyards are irrigated, and the scientifically timed application of precise amounts of water has become an important aspect of grape-growing and ripening. The lengthy fall harvest season, which can run from late August into early November, is marked by warm days and very cool nights. The 40 to 50 degree Fahrenheit daily temperature swings keep acids up as sugars rise, which means that in many vintages, no acidification is necessary. Alcohol levels for finished wines have risen, but are still below the numbers for California.

The exploration of Washington *terroir* is well underway, and the state actually has plantings of Cabernet as old or older than any in California, where vines have been ravaged by disease. Red Mountain in particular has proven itself as a spectacular region for Merlot and Cabernet, and the Red Mountain vineyards of Klipsun and Ciel du Cheval provide grapes to dozens of Washington's best boutique wineries.

Walla Walla has become an important tourist destination, with more than eighty wineries, 1,200 acres of vineyard, year-round recreational activities, and an active and fun-loving wine community. Pioneered in the early 1980s by Leonetti Cellar, L'Ecole No 41, and Woodward Canyon, the valley is now home to dozens of wineries producing small lots of rich, oaky red wines and ripe, succulent whites. Syrah does particularly well.

Eastern Washington has periodically suffered from arctic blasts that can devastate vineyards. The most recent, early in 2004, all but eliminated that year's harvest in Walla Walla. But much is being learned about Washington viticulture, and new plantings are better sited to survive the occasional frigid winters. Additionally, established vineyards are maturing, and older vines with deeper roots are far less likely to be killed by even severe cold.

Most of Washington's wineries produce fewer than two thousand cases of wine annually, and awareness of the state's best wines has been hampered by this lack of production. Additionally, there have been very few wineries large enough to produce soundly-made, inexpensive "supermarket" wines, the kind that help establish a national presence. The wines of Columbia Crest, Covey Run, and Precept brands are beginning to change that, challenging the huge California conglomerates with budget bottles that don't skimp on either character or quality.

Oregon

Unlike Washington, where vineyards are scattered throughout the east, most Oregon vineyards lie in the state's western half. They are somewhat protected from ocean fogs and cloud cover by the coastal mountain range. The farther south you go, the hotter it gets. In the Rogue Valley appellation, centered around the town of Ashland, Syrah and Cabernet can be ripened, though with rather tough, chewy tannins. But it is the Pinot Noirs of the northern Willamette valley that have brought Oregon to the attention of the world.

Vineyards of Domaine Serene, Dayton, Oregon.

Oregon became known as the Pinot Noir state at a time when decent Pinot was hard to come by outside of Burgundy. Pioneered by David Lett, David Adelsheim,

Dick Ponzi, and Dick Erath, Oregon Pinot in the early years was indeed Burgundian, elegant and light, with modest color and relatively low alcohol levels.

Over the years, as viticulture improved and winemakers learned new techniques, Oregon Pinot became thicker, darker, more jammy, and hot in the ripe years; and more tannic and earthy in the cool ones. Recently, as Pinot Noirs from California, New Zealand, and elsewhere have risen in quality, Oregon vintners have begun turning their attention to other varietals. The Willamette Valley's two hundred-plus wineries still predominantly produce Pinot, but some of the state's most interesting wines are coming from other grapes grown outside the region.

The big challenges for Oregon Pinot are two-fold. First, vintage variation is a fact of life, and wines can range from thin, harsh, and weedy to hot, ripe, and impenetrable. Unlike California and Washington, where vintages are far more consistent, Oregon vintners can expect something different every year. Hail, rain, extreme heat, humidity, drought, and vast temperature swings during harvest are the norm, not the exception.

To some degree, this is a good thing, because it suggests that Oregon, like a handful of other winemaking regions scattered across the globe, has the ability to put its own distinct stamp on its wines. The plus side of vintage variation is that each harvest is unique, and imparts specific, unique qualities to the wines of that vintage. The minus side is that not every vintage is all that good, especially where Pinot Noir is concerned.

The second challenge is that there is no longer a generally identifiable Oregon Pinot "style." Some vintners make elegant, light, tannic Pinots that require years to open up, while others make wines so dark and jammy, they are dead ringers for Syrah. And finally, while there are plenty of pricey, single-vineyard Pinots being produced, it is still difficult for consumers to find drinkable, good value, every day bottles.

Oregon's Rieslings and Gewürztraminers remain well-kept secrets. These are lively, juicy, floral, and fragrant wines that are always good value. The state's signature white is Pinot Gris, and it's made in a lush, fruity style that tastes of fresh-cut pears and goes easy on the new oak. The Chardonnays, once clumsy and fat, have dramatically improved with the introduction of Dijon clones.

Some producers have demonstrated remarkable success with grapes not generally associated with Oregon. Syrah is grown in the south, and makes a big, tannic, rough-hewn red wine. At Abacela in central Oregon, Tempranillo has proved surprisingly good, and the old-vine Zinfandels of Sineann, from an eastern Oregon vineyard, are superb. Oregon has added several new AVAs in the past couple of years, but what is most exciting are these new wines from different grapes that promise to open up Oregon to its full potential in the decades ahead.

Australia

Although Philip Schaffer was the first to plant a successful vineyard in Australia in 1791, it wasn't until the mid-nineteenth century that grape growing and viticulture was more widespread throughout South Australia, Victoria, and New South Wales. In the 1880s, however, phylloxera (see Glossary) spread through Victoria and New South Wales. South Australia's very stringent (and still existent) quarantine policy spared its vines from the louse and, to this day, the state is the seat of Australia's wine production.

Zinfandel vines of Cape Mentelle, Margaret River, Western Australia.

It's only been during the past twenty or so years that Australia has become known on the world stage as a premium wine-producing nation. It is now home to about 1,800 wineries and is the fourth-largest wine-exporting country (behind France, Italy, and Spain), with export sales topping $2.7 billion in 2004. The country's biggest export markets are the United States and the United Kingdom, though Australian wine is exported to over one hundred countries.

Australia is vast; at over 7.6 million square kilometers, it is roughly the size of the continental United States, but is home to only about 15 percent of America's population. In spite of its size, many wine drinkers outside Australia have it in their heads that Oz wines all taste the same. To characterize them all as broad-shouldered, plum- and berry-flavored, well-oaked wines that are high in alcohol is as short-sighted as saying that all Americans—from the Bronx to Alabama—have the same accent. With that in mind, here's a broad overview of some of the country's best-known winemaking regions, or Geographical Indications (GIs), and the wines for which each region is best known.

The general area around Perth, in the southwestern corner of Western Australia, is home to some of the country's most coveted, premium-quality wines. The Margaret River GI is the most renowned of the GIs in Western Australia. The region's maritime climate yields structured, age-worthy Cabernet Sauvignons, and some of the country's best Chardonnays. Sémillon and Sauvignon Blanc blends are successful here, too.

In South Australia, where most of Australia's wine is produced, most GIs are located within a drive of the port city of Adelaide. It is in this state that Shiraz flourishes—just about every winery makes one.

Clare Valley, home of Australia's best Riesling (all of which is sealed with a screwcap), is located about eighty-five miles north of Adelaide. It has an altitude of 400 to 500 meters above sea level, and benefits from cool evening breezes and warm summers. Barossa Valley, just southwest of Clare, is hot, dry, and flat, with summertime temperatures that can top 100 degrees Fahrenheit. Most of Australia's flagship Shirazes come from Barossa Valley. The wines are generally big and broad, with luscious, extracted plum and berry fruit. Grenache and Cabernet Sauvignon, too, are very good here. Eden Valley, just south of Barossa, succeeds with both reds and whites, but you'll find that its Rieslings, Chardonnays, and Viogniers are among the country's best.

Directly south of Adelaide are McLaren Vale and, to its east, the Adelaide Hills. Like Barossa Valley, McLaren Vale also specializes in Shiraz and Grenache (and to a lesser degree, Cabernet). The Vale's microclimates are varied—some areas are flat and hot, others cooler, yielding wines from one GI that can taste very different. Most McLaren Vale reds, though, are lush in the mid-palate, often with a silky, chalky feel. The Adelaide Hills, at an altitude of about 400 meters above sea level, specializes in wines that thrive in cooler climates: Sauvignon Blanc, Chardonnay, Pinot Noir, Riesling, and other aromatic whites. Other reds can thrive in the region's warmest sites. Coonawarra, even farther south from Adelaide, is famed for its terra rossa soils, from which yield long-lived Cabernet Sauvignon.

Though there are a number of winegrowing regions in the state of Victoria, the best known is the Yarra Valley, from whence come some very good Chardonnays and Pinot Noirs. Wines from this region are often delicate and understated, rather than powerful, which again proves just how broad the spectrum is on Australia's wine styles. Rutherglen, in northeastern Victoria, is home to the country's (and really, some of the world's) most renowned fortified Muscats. Tasmania, the island just south of Victoria, is home to some of Australia's coolest grape-growing sites. As such, Riesling, Chardonnay, and Pinot Noir thrive here; production of sparkling wines containing the latter two grapes is also a specialty.

Just north of Sydney in New South Wales lies the Hunter Valley, an area with hot temperatures moderated by mild maritime breezes, and rain in the months leading up to harvest. This is Sémillon country; the region's famed white wine is known for its long aging potential. Shiraz and Chardonnay are also very good here.

New Zealand

In recent years, the New Zealand wine industry has mushroomed in size like no other. New Zealand now boasts more than five hundred wineries in a country with a total human population of only four million. The reason behind this growth has been exports. From 1995 to 2005, United States imports of New Zealand wine went

Fairhall Downs Estate produces wine in the Brancott Valley, Marlborough, New Zealand.

from just over NZ$1 million to more than NZ$113 million. The result is that consumers in the United States are seeing more and more New Zealand wines on store shelves and restaurant wine lists. Thankfully, quality has remained generally excellent, thanks to a rigorous export certification process, a solid technological base, and a rapidly expanding understanding of viticulture.

NEW ZEALAND WINE REGIONS

Marlborough The engine driving New Zealand's growth, Marlborough wine production is dominated by Sauvignon Blanc. With its crisp, grassy, herbal-yet-tropical style, it has become the hallmark of New Zealand. Yet Marlborough is also capable of making other fine aromatic white wines, as well as Pinot Noir and Chardonnay.

Hawkes Bay Known for its Bordeaux-style reds from Merlot and Cabernet Sauvignon, which can be very fine in warm vintages, but excessively herbal in others. Alternative reds, such as Malbec and Syrah, are gaining in popularity, with Syrah in particular likely to emerge as a star.

Martinborough Together with the surrounding Wairarapa, Martinborough is Pinot Noir country. The wines marry cherry fruit with an often intense, wiry-herbal character that adds character and staying power.

Central Otago The world's southernmost winegrowing region has gained a reputation for its bold, dramatically fruity Pinot Noirs, but also makes some surprisingly good Rieslings.

Other important parts of New Zealand include Waipara for Riesling and Burgundy varieties, Gisborne for Chardonnay, and Nelson for a spectrum of grape varieties similar to Marlborough's.

Chile

Chile saw its original grapevines arrive with sixteenth-century Spanish missionaries, but the first semblance of a modern winemaking industry dates back to the early part of the nineteenth century, when a naturalist by the name of Claudio Gay imported about sixty varieties of grapes from France. In turn, some of these grapes were planted in the Maipo Valley, which encompasses the city of Santiago, and by the 1850s commercial wine existed.

From an American's perspective, Chilean wine started to make its mark in the 1970s, when protectionist restrictions were lifted by the military dictatorship headed by Augusto Pinochet. Almost immediately, exports spiked, with value-priced wines pouring into America as well as other countries. Some thirty years later, Chile is one of the world's most aggressive exporters; its wines make it to nearly one hundred countries around the globe, with shipments to the United States leading the way.

In many ways, the climate, geology, and geography of Chile are like that of western North America, but turned upside-down. Chile's north is a bone-dry desert, roughly equal to Baja California, only drier. The middle of the country is verdant and river-fed, with soils perfect for all sorts of agriculture,

Wine barrels in the cellars of Viña Luis Felipe Edwards, Chile.

not the least of which is grapes. So in that sense it's like California, Oregon, and Washington. And as one goes south it quickly gets colder and more rugged, not unlike British Columbia and eventually Alaska.

In the midsection of this 4,000-mile-long sliver of a country, there's a 500-mile chunk called the Central Valley, and within this valley there are a number of prime wine-growing regions. The most historic is Maipo, in which just about all grapes are grown. But it's Cabernet Sauvignon that has always been king in Maipo. Whether it's a simple everyday Maipo Cabernet like Cousiño-Macul's Antiguas Reservas or one of the country's best premium offerings like Concha y Toro's Don Melchor, a Maipo Cabernet is well worth hailing.

Other prominent wine regions include Aconcagua and Limari, the two northern frontiers of premium grape growing. There aren't many wineries there, but the wines are solid and true. Bordering Maipo to the west is the CasaBlanca Valley, first planted by Pablo Morandé and his family in the early 1990s. Cool and coastal, CasaBlanca and neighboring Leyda and San Antonio are prime spots for Chardonnay and Sauvignon Blanc but have trouble when it comes to producing ripe red wines.

South of Maipo is Rapel and its two parallel valleys: Cachapoal and Colchagua. Here the weather is warm, and the majority of grapes are red. Colchagua is arguably the leading region in Chile for red wines, and there's a plethora of big, burly wines based on Syrah, Cabernet Sauvignon, Merlot, Malbec, and Carmenère coming from Colchagua wineries including Montes, Casa Lapostolle, Viu Manent, MontGras, and Los Vascos.

Further south are the regions of Curicó and Maule. It was in Curicó that Miguel Torres of Spain set up shop in 1979 and introduced the then-revolutionary concept of steel-tank fermentation to Chile. To borrow a well-used phrase and apply it to how wine is now being made throughout the country: the rest is history.

Argentina

Argentina features a vaunted winemaking history that began some five hundred years ago when Spanish missionaries first arrived and planted vines. But it wasn't until about two hundred years ago that Argentina developed a commercial wine industry, largely centered in the province of Mendoza, located about four hundred miles directly west of Buenos Aires.

For all intents and purposes, Argentina's wine industry was until fairly recently geared toward domestic consumption. Nineteenth and early twentieth-century immigrants from Spain and Italy had a huge thirst for wine, and the vineyards that they planted along the western edge of the country, where the climate is dry, the temperatures are warm, and there's plenty of water available from the mighty Andes, produced copious amounts of varietal and blended reds that the Argentine population drank with nary a complaint.

To a large extent, that's still the case. Argentineans remain the primary consumers of their own wines. But as the global wine market began to take shape in the latter half of the twentieth century, Argentina refocused its winemaking and marketing efforts to highlight exports. Today, there are approximately one hundred wineries throughout Argentina that are sending their wines overseas. Mendoza, with its numerous subzones, remains front and center among wine regions, with areas like San Rafael, La Rioja, San Juan, Salta, and Cafayate vying for second chair.

Due to a pervasive hot, dry climate, it's safe to say that red wines outperform white wines in almost all parts of Argentina; although the higher one goes into the Andes, the cooler it gets and the crisper the white wines become. And with such deep Italian and Spanish roots running through the country's people, that makes sense.

Malbec, which was brought to Argentina from France some 150 years ago, has emerged as Argentina's signature grape. It is grown throughout the country, and while it varies in style, one can safely call it fruity, aromatic, and lush. In flatter, warmer vineyards, Malbec can be soft and simple, an easy wine for everyday drinking and blending.

But if taken into the foothills of the mountains or grown in old vineyards, it can be a wine of immense character.

Joining Malbec on the red roster is Cabernet Sauvignon, which is flavorful and serious when coming from top wineries like Terrazas de Los Andes, Catena Zapata, Norton, Cobos, or Chakana, to name several. Picked ripe, like in California and aged mostly in French oak barrels, Argentinean Cabernet has what it takes.

Other red grapes one frequently encounters are Bonarda and Sangiovese, both of which were brought over from Italy, as well as Merlot, Syrah, Tempranillo, and even some Pinot Noir.

Harvesting grapes in a vineyard of Peñaflor, Mendoza, Argentina.

Among white wines, one of Argentina's best and most distinctive offerings is Torrontes, an import from Galicia in Spain. Floral and occasionally exotic in scent and taste, Torrontes seems to do best in the more northern Salta region, where there's higher humidity and more rain than in Mendoza.

And as stated before, the Andean foothills are proving to be the prime spot for Chardonnay. At elevations of more than 3,000 feet above sea level, warm days and cool nights yield naturally fresh and properly acidic wines. Flavors of pineapple, green banana, and other tropical fruits are common among Argentina's modern-day Chardonnays.

Uruguay

Uruguay is South American's fourth-largest wine producer (behind Chile, Argentina, and Brazil), and, in global wine terms, is best described as an emerging market.

With a couple hundred years of grape-growing history to its name, and 135 years of commercial winemaking history, Uruguay has never quite caught on the way Argentina and Chile have. Nonetheless, many vinifera grapes, most imported from France, are grown in Uruguay, including Cabernet Sauvignon, Merlot, Pinot Noir, Riesling, and Gewürztraminer. That said, the calling-card grape for the country is Tannat, a rustic variety hailing from Madiran, in southwest France. Somewhat of a chameleon, Uruguayan Tannat can be made in a racier, fruity style or in a more international, barrel-aged style.

South Africa

After a slow start, South Africa's wines have reached international heights. The wines are sold at an impressively good value, and the country offers styles and tastes that are special and—importantly—enjoyable.

South Africa has been producing wine since the first vineyards were planted by the French in the seventeenth century, brought to the country by the Dutch governors of Cape Colony. At one time, the sweet wine of Constantia was the most prized in the world. For decades, South Africa, as part of the British Empire, sent shiploads of fortified wines to London.

This luxurious past can still be seen in the stunningly beautiful Cape vineyards, and the elegant, gabled Dutch Cape houses that form the centerpieces of many wine estates. But the future has also made its mark in South Africa's vineyards, where local winemakers (joined by an increasing number of European and American winemakers and investors) are creating a new generation of wines.

Boschendal Estate, Groot Drakenstein Valley, Franschhoek, Cape Province, South Africa.

The style, the character of the wines, is somewhere between California or Australia and Europe. Food friendly and equally elegant and powerful, there are many wines here for drinkers tired of alcoholic blockbusters.

All South Africa's vineyards are within an hour or three of Cape Town, in the southwest corner of the country. South Africa has its own appellation system, Wine of Origin, which is indicated on the label and on a government-issued neck sticker.

The most important quality wine areas are around the two cities of Stellenbosch and Paarl. All wine styles are made here: the country's greatest reds are from Stellenbosch, but Paarl's sub-district of Franschhoek runs a close second. Increasingly, other areas are being developed: the west coast, which makes great cooler-climate Sauvignon Blanc and red wines under the Darling and Swartland Wine of Origin, and the south coast at Walker Bay and Elgin, from which the country's best Pinot Noir comes.

The other famed quality area (although tiny in volume) is Constantia, almost in the suburbs of Cape Town. The original Cape vineyards now make impressive reds and whites in the country's most historic wine estates.

Larger-volume areas are further north and east than these classic heartland areas: Robertson, known for its Chardonnay, Worcester, for inexpensive volume wines, and Oliphants River, better known for reds and fortified wines.

South Africa's wine styles are evolving. Chenin Blanc, the local white workhorse grape, is also capable of making some impressive dry and sweet wines. Sauvignon Blanc has the potential to be more exciting than Chardonnay.

For reds, Pinotage, South Africa's own red grape (a cross between Pinot Noir and Cinsaut) still leaves wine critics divided, but can make great things, especially if found in Cape Blend wines (Pinotage blended with other red grapes). Shiraz is seen as the new hope for red wine, but Cabernet Sauvignon, Merlot, and Bordeaux blend wines are still the country's top reds.

Canada

The Canadian wine industry divides neatly in half. In eastern Canada, the Niagara Peninsula north of Lake Ontario produces the vast majority of the region's wines. The government-funded switch to vinifera vines in the early 1990s revolutionized the region, which produces roughly four-fifths of Canada's wine grapes. Though a wide range of varietal white and red wines are made, it is the region's ice wines, marketed in super-tall, slim, 375 ml bottles, that have brought it global acclaim. Meanwhile, British Columbia has been quietly building a substantial wine industry of its own, especially on the bluffs surrounding Lake Okanagan, where a compelling blend of wine and recreational tourism draws visitors year-round. Everything from Germanic Rieslings to Burgundian Pinots to Bordeaux-style red wines and even Syrah can be ripened here. More than one hundred wineries call British Columbia home, with more opening every month.

Greece

Greece's best, most distinctive wines are indigenous grape varieties that are unknown elsewhere. Moschofilero is Greece's answer to Pinot Grigio—a light, attractively fruity white that can be charming when cleanly made. Reds tend to be more rustic, whether made from Agiorgitiko or Xinomavro.

Hungary

Although home to the storied wines of Tokaji and Egri Bikaver (Bull's Blood), quality was stunted by the chaos that supplanted Communism. Western investment and heroic individual efforts are just beginning to bear fruit.

Bulgaria and Romania

As they prepare for admission to the European Union in 2007, these two contries have been upgrading their vineyards and wineries. Bulgaria has some 200,000 acres of vinifera vines in production, Romania has about the same. Look for good-value Chardonnays, Merlots, and Cabernets from Bulgaria in particular. Merlot and Cabernet show promise in Romania, along with indigenous reds such as Feteasca Neagra.

Croatia

Original homeland to Zinfandel—known on the Dalmatian coast as Crljenik Kasteljanski. Plavac Mali is a similar grape, making sometimes tough, tannic wines.

Israel

High-tech farming is a hallmark of Israeli agriculture and grape growing is no different, with carefully metered irrigation of international grape varieties the rule rather than the exception. A new generation of carefully sculpted reds is raising the bar.

Lebanon

For years, Lebanese wine was synonymous with Château Musar, but now other names have joined the Hochar family in making wine amidst the ruins. Reds show the most promise.

Slovenia

Bordering Italy's Collio region, Slovenia produces many of the same grape varieties, including pungent Sauvignon and classy Tocai, as well as blended whites.

CHAPTER SIX

Matching Wine and Food

IF YOU YOU THINK ABOUT MATCHING WINE and food flavors, you probably fall into one of two camps: foodie or wine enthusiast. Foodies concoct a menu and then think about what wine to open; while wine enthusiasts decide what lovely bottle they really want to drink, and *then* decide what food will be best.

Either approach works. Most of the time, we all do a little of each kind of thinking when planning wine and food pairings. The goal is the same: You want the wine and

food to complement, perhaps even improve, each other. The more you learn to differentiate flavors, the easier it becomes. You will find that you can intuitively sense how flavors will combine. So if you already love to cook, and know how to adjust your seasonings and sauces, you're halfway there. Conversely, if you already love wine, and understand how to analyze its various scents and flavors, you can approach your menu from that perspective.

Each season offers some opportunity, great or small, for the worlds of food and wine to do a graceful *pas de deux*. At its best, this goes well beyond merely "matching" the wine to the food; it becomes a performance in which two worlds collide, then merge, then harmonize and expand.

We all have individual sensitivities. These play a significant role in defining your food and wine preferences. Some people are more sensitive to bitterness or sweetness, others will easily pick up on the acid in food or wine. So the following guidelines are general, and should not be taken as hard and fast rules.

Successful food and wine matches are highly dependent upon these personal preferences. Yes, there are some classics—goat cheese and Sauvignon Blanc, for example. But the real fun is experimenting, to find for yourself which of the wines you happen to enjoy go best with which of the foods you like to serve.

Remember, you are looking for pleasure, not seeking perfection. Some people can't tolerate red wine, others think that all wine would be red if it could. So it's good to be flexible, and have several options ready to go with a given meal.

Wine flavors are derived from specific components: sugar, acid, fruit, tannin, and alcohol. Foods also have flavor components: fat, acid, salt, sugar, and bitter. The most successful food and wine matches feature complementary components, richness, and textures.

You can try for either a similar pairing or a contrasting one. For a pasta in a rich cream sauce, for example, you could cut through the creamy fat with a crisp, dry, un-oaked white wine. Or you could wrap the flavor of the wine around the richness of the sauce by choosing a big, ripe, soft Chardonnay or Roussanne/Marsanne blend.

A lot of our favorite foods, both meat and dairy products, have high levels of fat. Wine doesn't contain fat. So when planning a wine to go with fatty foods, remember that it has to balance that fat with acid, cut it with tannin, or match its richness with alcohol.

This is why a prime cut of steak tastes so good with a Cabernet-based wine. The beef's protein and fat softens up the wine's mouth-drying tannins. This sets up the tongue for the wine's fruit and berry and forest flavors to complement the smoky, meaty flavors of the steak.

Acid is another key element in both food and wine. In wine it adds nerve, freshness, and lift. It can do the same with food, as when lemon is squeezed on steamed vegetables. When looking for a wine to go with an acidic dish, you should make sure that the perceived acidity of the wine is at least equal to that of the food, or the wine will taste bland and washed out.

Salads are often a challenge for wine matching, but you can make it work if you moderate the acid in the dressing by cutting back on the lemon juice or vinegar. Try using some tangy, bitter greens, and offset them with herbal flavors from Sauvignon Blanc or Sémillon.

Next up: salt. Salty foods seem to limit your wine choices. Salt can make an oaky Chardonnay taste weird, strip the fruit right out of a red wine, and turn high alcohol wines bitter. It's so much easier to drink beer! But with a bit of imagination, you can conjure up some

remarkable combinations of salty foods and sweet wines. Bleu cheese and Sauternes is another one of the world's classic food and wine combos.

Sparkling wines are a home run with salty, fried foods. The carbonation and yeasty acids emulate beer and clean the salt from your palate, while adding more interesting textures and flavor nuances. Salt is also a principal flavor in briny seafood, such as oysters. Acidic wines clean out the salt and balance the rich ocean flavors of the oyster.

Sweet desserts and other sugary foods seem easy—just pull out a sweet wine—but beware. Here is where there is one rule that really needs to be observed.

There are degrees of sweetness. Some recipes will have just a hint of sugar, such as a fruit sauce served over a pork loin. This light, fruity sweetness can be matched very well with rich white wines such as Chardonnay. Higher alcohol tends to give an impression of sweetness, and balances the sugar in the sauce.

With desserts you must be certain that the wine tastes sweeter than the dessert; otherwise the dessert will strip the wine of its sweetness and render it bitter or tart.

Though red wine and chocolate is a combination often promoted by the wine industry, you have to be very careful about it. Use a bitter, dark chocolate and a red wine with some sweetness, such as a late-harvest Zinfandel, and it can be quite wonderful. But a sweet chocolate dessert and a dry red? Terrible!

What about bitter flavors? In some cultures, bitter flavors are prized, but most of the time they are to be avoided. Anything more than just a hint is likely to be perceived as unpleasant. In wine, bitterness usually results from unripe grapes, or a failure to get the stems and pips (seeds) out of the fermenting tank, or mismanaged barrels. When bitterness in wine meets bitterness in food, it acts the opposite of sugar. One does not cancel out the other; they merely combine.

As for matching textures, think light and heavy. Light foods are best with light wines; heavy foods with heavy wines. That's the safest way to go about it. A more adventurous path is to experiment with contrast: matching light foods to heavy wines and vice versa. This will require more testing, to keep the tension dynamic, and avoid having the lighter flavors over-shadowed by the heavy ones.

Glossary

Acidity: A naturally occurring component of every wine; the level of perceived sharpness; a key element to a wine's longevity; a leading determinant of balance.

Ageworthy: Wines whose general characteristics make it likely that they will improve with age.

Alcohol: The end product of fermentation; technically ethyl alcohol resulting from the interaction of natural grape sugars and yeast; generally above 12.5 percent in dry table wines.

Alsace: A highly regarded wine region in eastern France renowned for dry and sweet wines made from Riesling, Gewürztraminer, Pinot Blanc, Pinot Gris, and others.

Amarone: A succulent higher-alcohol red wine hailing from the Veneto region in northern Italy; made primarily from Corvina grapes dried on racks before pressing.

AOC: *Appellation d'Origine Contrôlée*, a French term for a denominated, governed wine region, such as Margaux or Nuits-St.-Georges.

Aroma: A scent that's a component of the bouquet or nose; i.e. cherry is an aromatic component of a fruity bouquet.

AVA: American Viticultural Area; a denominated American wine region approved by the Bureau of Alcohol, Tobacco, and Firearms.

Bacchus: The Roman god of wine, known as Dionysus in ancient Greece; a hybrid white grape from Germany.

Balance: The level of harmony between acidity, tannins, fruit, oak, and other elements in a wine; a perceived quality that is more individual than scientific.

Barrel Fermented: A process by which wine (usually white) is fermented in oak barrels rather than in stainless steel tanks; a richer, creamier, oakier style of wine.

Barrique: French for "barrel," generally a barrel of 225 liters.

Beaujolais: A juicy, flavorful red wine made from Gamay grapes grown in the region of the same name.

Beaujolais Nouveau: The first Beaujolais wine of the harvest; its annual release date is the third Thursday in November.

Blanc de Blancs: The name for Champagne made entirely from Chardonnay grapes.

Blanc de Noirs: The name for Champagne made entirely from red grapes, either Pinot Noir or Pinot Meunier, or both.

Blend: The process whereby two or more grape varieties are combined after separate fermentation; common blends include Côtes de Rhône and red and white Bordeaux.

Blush: A wine made from red grapes but which appears pink or salmon in color because the grape skins were removed from the fermenting juice before more color could be imparted; more commonly referred to as Rosé.

Bodega: Spanish for winery; literally "room where barrels are stored."

Body: The impression of weight on one's palate; "light," "medium," and "full" are common body qualifiers.

Bordeaux: A city on the Garonne River in southwest France; a large wine-producing region with more than a dozen subregions; a red wine made mostly from Cabernet Sauvignon, Merlot, and Cabernet Franc; a white wine made from Sauvignon Blanc and Sémillon.

Botrytis Cinerea: (also Noble Rot) A beneficial mold that causes grapes to shrivel and sugars to concentrate, resulting in sweet, unctuous wines; common botrytis wines include Sauternes, Tokay, and German Beerenauslese.

Bouquet: The sum of a wine's aromas; how a wine smells as a whole; a key determinant of quality.

Breathe: The process of letting a wine open up via the introduction of air.

Brettanomyces: An undesirable yeast that reeks of sweaty saddle scents.

Brix: A scale used to measure the level of sugar in unfermented grapes. Multiplying brix by 0.55 will yield a wine's future alcohol level.

Brut: A French term used to describe the driest Champagnes.

Burgundy: A prominent French wine region stretching from Chablis in the north to Lyons in the south; Pinot Noir is the grape for red Burgundy, Chardonnay for white.

Cabernet Franc: A red grape common to Bordeaux; characteristics include an herbal, leafy flavor and a soft, fleshy texture.

Cabernet Sauvignon: A powerful, tannic red grape of noble heritage; the base grape for many red Bordeaux and most of the best red wines from California, Washington, Chile, and South Africa; capable of aging for decades.

Cap: Grape solids like pits, skins, and stems that rise to the top of a tank during fermentation; what gives red wines color, tannins, and weight.

Carbonic Maceration: A wine-making process in which whole grapes are sealed in a fermenter with carbon dioxide and left to ferment without yeast and grape crushing.

Cava: Spanish for "cellar," but also a Spanish sparkling wine made in the traditional Champagne style from Xarello, Macabeo, and Parellada grapes.

Chablis: A town and wine region east of Paris known for steely, minerally Chardonnay.

Champagne: A denominated region northeast of Paris in which Chardonnay, Pinot Noir, and Pinot Meunier grapes are made into sparkling wine.

Chaptalization: The process of adding sugar to fermenting grapes in order to increase alcohol.

Chardonnay: Arguably the best and most widely planted white wine grape in the world.

Château: French for "castle;" an estate with its own vineyards.

Chenin Blanc: A white grape common in the Loire Valley of France.

Chianti: A scenic, hilly section of Tuscany known for fruity red wines made mostly from Sangiovese grapes.

Claret: An English name for red Bordeaux.

Clos: Pronounced "Cloh," this French word once applied only to vineyards surrounded by walls.

Color: A key determinant of a wine's age and quality; white wines grow darker in color as they age while red wines turn brownish orange.

Cooperative: A winery owned jointly by multiple grape growers.

Corked: A wine with musty, mushroomy aromas and flavors resulting from a cork tainted by TCA (trichloroanisol).

Crianza: A Spanish term for a red wine that has been aged in oak barrels for at least one year.

Cru: A French term for ranking a wine's inherent quality, i.e. Cru Bourgeois, Cru Classé, Premier Cru, and Grand Cru.

Decant: The process of transferring wine from a bottle to another holding vessel. The purpose is generally to aerate a young wine or to separate an older wine from any sediment.

Denominación de Origen: Spanish for appellation of origin; like the French AOC or Italian DOC.

Denominazione di Origine Controllata: Italian for a controlled wine region; similar to the French AOC or Spanish DO.

Disgorge: The process by which final sediments are removed from traditionally made sparkling wines prior to the adding of the dosage.

Dosage: A sweetened spirit added at the very end to Champagne and other traditionally made sparkling wines. It determines whether a wine is brut, extra dry, dry, or semisweet.

Douro: A river in Portugal as well as the wine region famous for producing Port wines.

Dry: A wine containing no more than 0.2 percent unfermented sugar.

Earthy: A term used to describe aromas and flavors that have a certain soil-like quality.

Enology: The science of wine production; an enologist is a professional winemaker; an enophile is someone who enjoys wine.

Fermentation: The process by which sugar is transformed into alcohol; how grape juice interacts with yeast to become wine.

Filtration: The process by which wine is clarified before bottling.

Fining: Part of the clarification process whereby elements are added to the wine, i.e. egg whites, in order to capture solids prior to filtration.

Fortified Wine: A wine in which brandy is introduced during fermentation; sugars and sweetness are high due to the suspended fermentation.

Fumé Blanc: A name created by Robert Mondavi to describe dry Sauvignon Blanc.

Gamay: A red grape exceedingly popular in the Beaujolais region of France.

Gewürztraminer: A sweet and spicy white grape popular in eastern France, Germany, Austria, northern Italy, and California.

Graft: A vineyard technique in which the bud-producing part of a grapevine is attached to an existing root.

Gran Reserva: A Spanish term used for wines that are aged in wood and bottles for at least five years prior to release.

Grand Cru: French for "great growth;" the very best vineyards.

Green: A term used to describe underripe, vegetal flavors in a wine.

Grenache: A hearty, productive red grape popular in southern France as well as in Spain, where it is called Garnacha.

Grüner Veltliner: A white grape popular in Austria that makes lean, fruity, racy wines.

Haut: A French word meaning "high." It applies to quality as well as altitude.

Hectare: A metric measure equal to 10,000 square meters or 2.47 acres.

Hectoliter: A metric measure equal to 100 liters or 26.4 gallons.

Herbaceous: An aroma or flavor similar to green; often an indication of underripe grapes or fruit grown in a cool climate.

Hollow: A term used to describe a wine that doesn't have depth or body.

Hybrid: The genetic crossing of two or more grape types; common hybrids include Müller-Thurgau and Bacchus.

Ice Wine: From the German *eiswein*, this is a wine made from frozen grapes; Germany, Austria, and Canada are leading ice wine producers.

Jeroboam: An oversized bottle equal to six regular 750 ml bottles.

Kabinett: A German term for a wine of quality; usually the driest of Germany's best Rieslings.

Kosher: A wine made according to strict Jewish rules under rabbinical supervision.

Labrusca: Grape types native to North America, such as Concord and Catawba.

Late Harvest: A term used to describe dessert wines made from grapes left on the vines for an extra long period, often until botrytis has set in.

Lees: Heavy sediment left in the barrel by fermenting wines; a combination of spent yeast cells and grape solids.

Legs: A term used to describe how wine sticks to the inside of a wineglass after drinking or swirling.

Library Wines: Wines kept by the bottler as a reference of previous wines bottled.

Loire: A river in central France as well as a wine region famous for Chenin Blanc, Sauvignon Blanc, and Cabernet Franc.

Maceration: The process of allowing grape juice and skins to ferment together, thereby imparting color, tannins, and aromas.

Madeira: A fortified wine that has been made on a Portuguese island off the coast of Morocco since the fifteenth century.

Maderized: Stemming from the word Madeira, this term means oxidization in a hot environment.

Magnum: A bottle equal to two regular 750 ml bottles.

Malbec: A hearty red grape of French origin now exceedingly popular in Argentina.

Malolactic Fermentation: A secondary fermentation, often occurring in barrels, whereby harsher malic acid is converted into creamier lactic acid.

Médoc: A section of Bordeaux on the west bank of the Gironde Estuary known for great red wines; Margaux, St. Estèphe, and Pauillac are three leading AOCs in the Médoc.

Merlot: A lauded red grape popular in Bordeaux and throughout the world; large amounts of Merlot exist in Italy, the United States, South America, and elsewhere.

Must: Crushed grapes about to go or going through fermentation.

Nebbiolo: A red grape popular in the Piedmont region of northwest Italy; the grape that yields both Barolo and Barbaresco.

Négociant: A French term for a person or company that buys wines from others and then labels it under his or her own name; stems from the French word for "shipper."

Noble Rot: *see Botrytis Cinerea.*

Nose: Synonymous with "bouquet;" the sum of a wine's aromas.

Oaky: A term used to describe woody aromas and flavors; butter, popcorn, and toast notes are found in "oaky" wines.

Organic: Grapes grown without the aid of chemical-based fertilizers, pesticides, or herbicides.

Oxidized: A wine that is no longer fresh because it was exposed to too much air.

pH: An indication of a wine's acidity expressed by how much hydrogen is in it.

Phylloxera: A voracious vine louse that over time has destroyed vineyards in Europe and California.

Piedmont: An area in northwest Italy known for Barolo, Barbaresco, Barbera, Dolcetto, and Moscato.

Pinot Blanc: A white grape popular in Alsace, Germany, and elsewhere.

Pinot Gris: Also called Pinot Grigio, this is a grayish-purple grape that yields a white wine with a refreshing character.

Pinot Noir: The prime red grape of Burgundy, Champagne, and Oregon.

Pinotage: A hybrid between Pinot Noir and Cinsault that's grown almost exclusively in South Africa.

Plonk: A derogatory name for cheap, poor-tasting wine.

Pomace: The mass of skins, pits, and stems left over after fermentation; used to make grappa in Italy and marc in France.

Port: A sweet, fortified wine made in the Douro Valley of Portugal and aged in the coastal town of Vila Nova de Gaia; variations include Vintage, Tawny, Late Bottled Vintage, Ruby, White, and others.

Premier Cru: French for "first growth;" a high-quality vineyard but one not as good as Grand Cru.

Press: The process by which grape juice is extracted prior to fermentation; a machine that extracts juice from grapes.

Primeur (en): A French term for wine sold while it is sill in the barrels; known as "futures" in English-speaking countries.

Pruning: The annual vineyard chore of trimming back plants from the previous harvest.

Racking: The process of moving wine from barrel to barrel, while leaving sediment behind.

Reserva: A Spanish term for a red wine that has spent at least three years in barrels and bottles before release.

Reserve: A largely American term indicating a wine of higher quality; it has no legal meaning.

Rhône: A river in southwest France surrounded by villages producing wines mostly from Syrah; the name of the wine-producing valley in France.

Riddling: The process of rotating Champagne bottles in order to shift sediment toward the cork.

Riesling: Along with Chardonnay, one of the top white grapes in the world; most popular in Germany, Alsace, and Austria.

Rioja: A well-known region in Spain known for traditional red wines made from the Tempranillo grape.

Rosé: French for "pink," used to describe a category of refreshing wines that are pink in color but are made from red grapes.

Sancerre: An area in the Loire Valley known mostly for wines made from Sauvignon Blanc.

Sangiovese: A red grape native to Tuscany; the base grape for Chianti, Brunello di Montalcino, Morellino di Scansano, and others.

Sauternes: A sweet Bordeaux white wine made from botrytized Sémillon and Sauvignon Blanc.

Sauvignon Blanc: A white grape planted throughout the world; increasingly the signature wine of New Zealand.

Sémillon: A plump white grape popular in Bordeaux and Australia; the base for Sauternes.

Sherry: A fortified wine from a denominated region in southwest Spain; styles include fino, manzanilla, oloroso, and amontillado.

Shiraz: The Australian name for Syrah; also used in South Africa and sparingly in the United States.

Silky: A term used to describe a wine with an especially smooth mouthfeel.

Solera: The Spanish system of blending wines of different ages to create a harmonious end product; a stack of barrels holding wines of various ages.

Sommelier: Technically a wine steward, but one potentially with a great degree of wine knowledge as well as a diploma of sorts in wine studies.

Spicy: A term used to describe certain aromas and flavors that may be sharp, woody, or sweet.

Split: A quarter-bottle of wine; a single-serving bottle equal to 175 milliliters.

Steely: A term used to describe an extremely crisp, acidic wine that was not aged in barrels.

Stemmy: A term used to describe harsh, green characteristics in a wine.

Super Tuscan: A red wine from Tuscany that is not made in accordance with established DOC rules; often a blended wine of superior quality containing Cabernet Sauvignon and/or Merlot.

Supple: A term used to describe smooth, balanced wines.

Syrah: A red grape planted extensively in the Rhône Valley of France, Australia, and elsewhere; a spicy, full, and tannic wine that usually requires aging before it can be enjoyed.

Table Wine: A term used to describe wines of between 10 and 14 percent alcohol; in Europe, table wines are those that are made outside of regulated regions or by unapproved methods.

Tannins: Phenolic compounds that exist in most plants; in grapes, tannins are found primarily in the skins and pits; tannins are astringent and provide structure to a wine; over time, tannins die off, making wines less harsh.

Tempranillo: The most popular red grape in Spain; common in Rioja and Ribera del Duero.

Terroir: A French term for the combination of soil, climate, and all other factors that influence the ultimate character of a wine.

Tokay: A dessert wine made in Hungary from dried Furmint grapes.

Trichloroanisole (TCA): A natural compound that at higher levels can impart "musty" flavors and aromas to wines, other beverages and foods. Wines that contain TCA at a detectable level are described as either being "corked" or having "corkiness," a damp, musty smell from a tainted cork.

Trocken: German for "dry."

Varietal: A wine made from just one grape type and named after that grape; the opposite of a blend.

Varietal Character: The distinct flavors, aromas, and other characteristics of each type of grape used to make wine.

Veneto: A large wine-producing region in northern Italy.

Vin Santo: Sweet wine from Tuscany made from late-harvest Trebbiano and Malvasia grapes.

Viticulture: The science and business of growing wine grapes.

Vintage: A particular year in the wine business; a specific harvest.

Viognier: A fragrant, powerful white grape grown in the Rhône Valley of France and elsewhere.

Volatile Acidity (VA): The development or presence of naturally occurring organic acids (acetic acid) in wine.

Yeast: Organisms that issue enzymes that trigger the fermentation process; yeasts can be natural or commercial.

Yield: The amount of grapes harvested in a particular year.

Zinfandel: A popular grape in California of disputed origin; scientists say it is related to grapes in Croatia and southern Italy.

PHOTOGRAPHY CREDITS